# WHY WHO CLEANS COUNTS

## What Housework Tells Us about American Family Life

Shannon N. Davis and Theodore N. Greenstein

ℙ

First published in Great Britain in 2020 by

Policy Press
University of Bristol
1-9 Old Park Hill
Bristol
BS2 8BB
UK
t: +44 (0)117 954 5940
pp-info@bristol.ac.uk
www.policypress.co.uk

North America office:
Policy Press
c/o The University of Chicago Press
1427 East 60th Street
Chicago, IL 60637, USA
t: +1 773 702 7700
f: +1 773-702-9756
sales@press.uchicago.edu
www.press.uchicago.edu

British Library Cataloguing in Publication Data
A catalogue record for this book is available from the British Library

Library of Congress Cataloging-in-Publication Data
A catalog record for this book has been requested

978-1-4473-3674-7 hardback
978-1-4473-3675-4 paperback
978-1-4473-3677-8 ePub
978-1-4473-3676-1 ePDF

Cover design by Robin Hawes
Front cover image: iStock/penguenstok

For Alexandra, my sunshine, Miles, my twinkle
star, and Frank, my guiding light.
S.N.D.

For my father, Jack Greenstein, who passed away during
the writing of this book. May his memory be a blessing.
T.N.G.

# Contents

# List of figures and tables

## Figures

## Tables

# Acknowledgments

This book is the product of a collaboration that originated in 1998 when Davis began graduate studies at North Carolina State University. Greenstein's research on housework was at the cutting edge and provided Davis with a theoretical and methodological framework from which to begin her own intellectual pursuits. Greenstein's own dissertation work in 1976 was itself an investigation into the influence of power dynamics on relationship behavior. The resulting research that we have produced since Davis began graduate school is an example of the transformative intellectual relationship that mentors and mentees can develop when ideas are valued reciprocally. This book is therefore but one of many successful collaborations between us, but one of which we are especially proud as it is the first research monograph that either of us has produced.

We thank the *Journal of Family Theory & Review* for publishing our special issue in 2013 (Volume 5, Issue 2), where we worked out our original ideas around the connections between power and housework, and Wiley for the license to use parts of our own article from that special issue in Chapters 1 and 2 (Volume 5, Issue 2, pp 63–71). We also thank the American Sociological Association for the chance to organize a panel at the 2012 Annual Meeting from which the *Journal of Family Theory & Review* special issue was born. We thank Policy Press for their support and encouragement, as well as patience, as this book was produced. We thank our editors and the press staff, especially Victoria Pittman, Isobel Bainton, Shannon Kneis, and Helen Davis, for their interest, their ideas, their insight, and their perspective, as well as their patience.

We thank Karen Nylund-Gibson, who superbly taught the 2017 Summer Quantitative Methods Series workshop at Portland State University on latent class analysis (LCA). Davis attended this workshop to develop the specific skills for the latent profile analysis (LPA) and latent trajectory analysis (LTA) reported in this book.

Thanks also go to Lisa Pearce, with whom Davis worked as a postdoctoral fellow at the Carolina Population Center. Conversations with Pearce when her book with Melinda Denton using LCA, *A faith of their own*, was in its early stages impacted the direction of this project, both conceptually and methodologically. Our project owes a debt to Lisa and Melinda for providing a clear roadmap to follow when thinking about understanding hidden patterns in social life.

We thank our home institutions and local colleagues for their support. Davis is appreciative of the Department of Sociology and Anthropology, the Center for Social Science Research, and the College of Humanities and Social Sciences Dean's Office at George Mason University as she worked for at least one semester in each unit during the writing of this book. The colleagues in these units were supportive, critical, and sympathetic at all the right times and always knew when coffee was needed. Conversations with Angie Hattery, Amy Best, Jim Witte, and Joe Scimecca were important sources of guidance. Graduate and undergraduate students over many semesters provided intellectual inspiration and critique as the book was completed, with special thanks to Emma Quach (University of Massachusetts—Boston) and Ray Sin (University of Illinois—Chicago) for their methodological inspiration in their dissertations. Greenstein completed some of the work for this volume while on a research leave granted by the College of Humanities and Social Sciences and received technology and software support from the Department of Sociology and Anthropology of North Carolina State University.

Finally, we thank our own families. Davis cannot thank enough Frank, Alexandra, and Miles for their unwavering love, encouragement, and patience, and for being the constant source of purpose for this book. Partnership is hard and is hard work, and Frank is a true partner in life, love, and parenthood. He is also a fabulous problem-solver and technical advisor, including but not limited to constructing the optimal remote working arrangements for the book's data analysis. Alexandra and Miles are the future and it is for them, and their generation, that this book is written. The women and men of tomorrow need role models for how to live that provide fair opportunities for all individuals to become their true best selves without being forced into relationships that truncate their potential. The possibilities nascent in Alex and Miles (and all other children) deserve the chance to fully blossom. Greenstein thanks Lori, Rachel, J.J. and Sam for their support while working on this book.

# What do we know about housework?

## Introduction

In August 2011, *Time* magazine published a story entitled "Chore wars" (Konigsberg, 2011), accompanied by a splashy front-page graphic, which drew attention to the amount of housework that women and men in the U.S. perform. When considering both paid labor (that is, men's and women's market work) and unpaid labor (non-market work, principally housework), the story found that women and men had relatively similar amounts of total work time. This distinction—that is, examining combined paid and unpaid labor hours as opposed to unpaid labor only—was lost on readers and, judging by the online comments responding to the story, was instead met with wide skepticism in the U.S. The story flew in the face of conventional wisdom: that housework is women's work and that while men are doing more than in the past, the burden of housework continues to fall to women. More importantly to readers, the story did not reflect their own lives. Average couples may be more equal in their (house) work time but readers were not average. Women lamented how much work they performed, and men were either silent or noted that their wife did the housework.

From our perspective, this cover story was interesting not due to the author's use of her own experiences of a changed division of paid and unpaid labor over time (which made for an interesting read in the popular press), but because of the sociological research cited throughout the story that explained the social factors in the U.S. that had underpinned women's increased labor-market participation and men's increases in housework (particularly in childcare). Indeed, much of the discussion in the article was around parents and childcare rather than the tasks that are connected to cooking, cleaning, and laundry, where evidence notes true disparities lie.[1] However, the print, broadcast, and online media responses to discussions around housework gave us pause. As scholars who have studied housework for decades, we believed that the public discussions were reflections of the private struggles over the changing responsibilities that women and men have in contributing to the household. We wanted to systematically investigate whether and how housework could be seen as a proxy for power dynamics in a couple, reflecting the struggles that couples negotiate around changing gender norms in the U.S.—and thus this project was born.

This introductory chapter provides a general overview of what we hope to accomplish in this book. We begin by presenting the two logics behind studying the division of labor: the cynical (doing and publishing research on housework is a good career strategy for academics); and the serious (doing housework is familiar to all of us and it is an inescapable part of our daily lives). We provide a general overview of the theoretical explanations for the division of housework and then explain our empirical investigation into the division of labor in U.S. couples that is the core of the book.

## Why study housework?

Why would researchers, including us, study something so mundane as housework? Why would researchers focus on trying to understand something so private and boring? Who cares who cleans the house? We will start with the academic answers to these questions. On the one hand, studying housework has been a very fruitful line of inquiry for researchers both in the U.S. and globally. Social scientists have been investigating the division of household labor in the U.S. since the 1960s. Beginning with Blood and Wolfe (1960), researchers have been studying married couples and how they run their homes. As families in the U.S. have become more diverse, and/or scholarly attention has been paid to diverse families, research has begun to focus on the division of household labor across a variety of households: cohabiting couples, stepfamilies, intergenerational families, families with children, immigrant families, families that differ by the race of the adults (black versus white families), and so on. Research has become comparative and historical. Scores of researchers have contributed to the ever-evolving theoretical and empirical conversation on the division of household labor. Figure 1.1 documents the trend in research scholarship that has examined housework over the last half-century. Therefore, one reason to study housework is that, for a researcher, it is a fruitful line of inquiry.

Another, less cynical, reason to study housework is that it is so mundane and familiar. We can all relate to research on housework. The findings resonate with us, as well as with the broader public, because

2

**Figure 1.1:** Published articles on household labor, 1960–2015

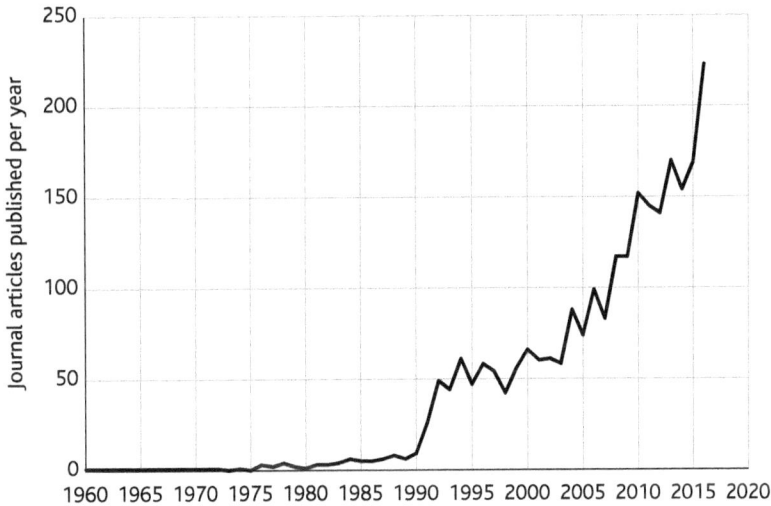

unlike some other fields of inquiry, everyone has experience with housework. Perhaps we had chores as children, or perhaps we assign chores to our kids. We saw our parents, largely our mothers, doing housework when we lived in their homes, and when we moved out, we had to figure out how to make our new living space clean, laundry done, food prepared, and bills paid. Maybe we were lucky enough and could afford to hire someone to do most of these tasks, and maybe that was the case in our family of origin. However, the management of the performance of these tasks is still housework. Furthermore, when we partnered with a significant other, task allocation had to be negotiated, and renegotiated over time. Therefore, it is no wonder that we study housework; it is a mundane and routine part of people's daily lives.

The familiarity of the tasks brings with it a ready-made audience, and that this potential audience will want to hear about our findings also leads us to study housework. People are interested in housework. For example, if you do the grocery shopping in your household, you may find it hard to avoid the magazines in the checkout aisles. Quite often, these magazines (targeted largely toward women) feature a story on housework: how to get husbands and children to do more; how to save time; basically, how to do less yourself. As noted earlier, housework is a constant source of interest for the popular media, as evidenced by the August 2011 cover story in *Time* magazine (Konigsberg, 2011) discussing similarities in women's and men's overall work hours (similar to an argument subsequently advanced in scholarly journals by England [2011]). Why do stories like this captivate the public? We believe that they captivate for one of the other reasons that we continue to study housework: relatively high proportions of individuals believe that, overall, housework is not in and of itself enjoyable and should thus be avoided. Indeed, family scholars have generally assumed that "housework is viewed negatively by both women and men and that they are therefore motivated to reduce their share of it" (Shelton and John, 1996: 304). While a few tasks (for example, cooking and gardening) are perceived as pleasant or gratifying by some, it is clear that, generally speaking, most people do not feel that housework is an enjoyable activity. So, if housework tasks are not enjoyable, why do people do them? What can explain why someone would want to spend time on an unpleasant task? Does the fact that housework tasks are necessary to the maintenance of a household change the reasoning behind why someone would perform work that they generally may find unpleasant? What can explain how and by whom the tasks that are deemed to be largely necessary to the maintenance of a household are completed? These questions, or some variant thereof, are at the core of this book.

We are arguing that by studying housework, something so mundane and familiar but yet so widely disliked, we can learn something about relationships. More specifically, the negotiation and renegotiation of the division of household labor can provide insights into relationship dynamics more broadly. Blood and Wolfe (1960) began the investigation into the division of household labor by discussing power dynamics and their correlates. We contend that one key reason that scholars should study housework, specifically inequality in the performance of housework, is the insights that can be gained regarding power and equity in intimate relationships. We are not arguing that insights about power are the *only* reason that scholars should study housework, but it certainly is an important one. Indeed, the study of housework has illuminated much about other facets of intimate relationships, that is, the importance of the concepts of fairness and justice in relationships (Major, 1987; DeMaris and Longmore, 1996; Greenstein, 1996, 2009; Kluwer et al, 2002; Davis, 2010). Furthermore, while these issues are also relevant to the broader social-scientific discourse on relationships, power as a concept has more purchase when staking general theoretical claims.

Contemporary Western marriages specifically, but intimate relationships more broadly, are typically framed as companionate (Coontz, 2006): spouses/significant others are seen as friends and partners. Contemporary Western societies tout their egalitarian social structures, so how is it that women consistently do more housework than do men? What are the social contexts, both local and structural, that facilitate greater equality? These questions ask about how individuals are able to work against the status quo *and* how individuals are able to maintain the status quo. These are questions about power and equity.

## Studying power through housework

Scholars have been theorizing about the gendered nature of power for decades (Connell, 1987; Chafetz, 1988); however, the usefulness of this theorizing has typically been limited to explaining what *was* (a description of the past) rather than predicting what may be. Kilbourne et al (2012: 694) suggested that "cultural processes of valuation are gendered; because women are devalued, social roles (including occupations) and skills that are associated with women are culturally devalued relative to those associated with men." Thus, housework itself is devalued because it has traditionally been associated with women. This book develops an argument about the ways in which housework has become a proxy for understanding the relationship between gender and power in heterosexual couples. We will argue that notions of equity are not only intertwined with latent (also referred to as hidden or covert) power and overt power, but also explicitly gendered. We are not the first scholars to make these types of claims, but we hope that by situating the conversation about housework as part of the conceptual conversation around power, we can encourage a refocusing of theoretical and empirical writing around housework. The hope is that renewed investigations will tell us about inequalities in many kinds of intimate relationships, not just married heterosexual couples, thus infusing the conversation about power and intimate relationships in the broader social science enterprise.

## Background: what do we already know about housework?

Journals have been publishing review articles documenting the current state of understanding on the division of household labor since the 1980s (Thompson and Walker, 1989; Shelton and John, 1996; Coltrane, 2000; Bianchi and Milkie, 2010; Lachance-Grzela and Bouchard, 2010). The structure of those review articles is quite consistent: the main theoretical approaches to understanding the division of household labor are defined; empirical evidence is provided for each approach; new lines of inquiry since the last review article are discussed; and directions for future research are presented. Given all of this reviewing, what do we know about the division of household labor? In the following, we describe the theoretical frameworks most often used to examine the division of household labor in order to clarify how power has and has *not* been invoked in these prominent explanations.

The main theoretical frameworks utilized fall into two main categories: resource-based and social-psychological/symbolic perspectives. Resource-based perspectives include those that investigate the effects of time availability and income (both absolute and relative), largely focusing on women, to determine what factors in women's lived experiences lead them to perform less housework. Sometimes, the research also asks what leads men to perform more housework. However, the goal of these studies is to understand how structural and material resources can be and are utilized as mechanisms through which women (and men) negotiate the amount of dreaded household tasks that they perform. Resource-based perspectives have found large support within the empirical literature, although much debate has recently ensued regarding the changing efficacy of these theoretical perspectives over time (Killewald and Gough, 2010; England, 2011; Kluwer, 2011; Risman, 2011; Sullivan, 2011). One empirical point, however, is unquestionably clear: "women cannot easily buy their way to equality with men when it comes to household labor responsibilities" (Killewald and Gough, 2010: 1001).

Social-psychological and symbolic/interpretive perspectives take into consideration the ways in which attitudes, values, beliefs, and expectations influence the performance of housework. Given that the division of housework is gendered, these perspectives tend to focus on either gender as a performance or the beliefs about gendered relationships (and the perceptions of fairness thereof) as the key explanatory factors for the performance of housework. Other research has looked for other social-psychological mechanisms that may or may not be correlated with gender as explanations for the division of housework. For example, Kluwer et al's (1996, 1997) work on challenging the status quo provides powerful evidence for how and why the division of household labor remains gendered, though the theoretical mechanisms tested in the research are not about gender per se. Hence, theorizing about housework does not necessarily have to intertwine gender and housework performance, though explanations have previously generally done so. What we want to bring to the fore is the implicit invocation of power when talking about gendered explanations for inequalities in the division of household labor, and to do so, more needs to be said about power in relationships.

## The structure of the book

The remainder of the book builds on the aforementioned claims that housework, gender, and power are intertwined in ways that can be documented within heterosexual couples in the U.S. In Chapter 2, we provide a review of the theoretical and empirical scholarship that has studied housework, and document how power dynamics have been integral to both strands of scholarship. In Chapter 3, we situate the National Study of Families and Households (NSFH) as a data source into the appropriate social and historical context, and present a description of the sample used in our analyses. Chapter 4 documents the core of our empirical analysis. Using couple data from the NSFH (Wave 1), we employ latent profile analysis to describe categories, or classes, of couples. Our analysis finds that couples fall into five categories: Ultra-Traditional, Traditional, Transitional Husbands, Egalitarian, and Egalitarian High Workload. Chapter 4 presents the profiles of each of these classes of couples based upon their joint division of labor. This analysis is unique in that we use self-reported data from each spouse in order to document patterns across the 3,906 couples for whom we have complete data.

Who is in each of the five housework classes? Chapter 5 describes each of the classes based upon couple and individual demographic characteristics, paying particular attention to how measures of power are distributed across the classes.

Chapter 6 examines a key component of our argument, namely, whether there are patterns across the five classes in other behavioral as well as attitudinal measures of power. In this chapter, we investigate spousal preferences for their own and their spouse's labor-market hours as a measure of being able to enact power. We also examine reported conflict, disagreements, and intimate partner violence, all behaviors that reflect power dynamics in a couple. These findings provide important evidence for our argument that understanding housework dynamics can provide insights into other dynamics in couples and can thus potentially be useful for practitioners working with families in crisis.

Do couples maintain their division of labor over time? Do they become more traditional or egalitarian as they age? Chapter 7 reports the results of a latent trajectory analysis examining stability and change in class membership over time. Using data from Waves 1 and 2 of the NSFH, we document change and stability in class membership. We describe the couple- and individual-level characteristics associated with both change and stability, as well as the new class profiles in Wave 2.

To highlight the value of our approach of using housework to understand power in families, we examine how changes or stability in housework over the life course are connected to changes or stability in key characteristics that reflect power in Chapter 8. We document how changes in class membership are connected with changes in labor-market participation, personal preferences for labor-market participation between spouses, income and relative income, and other measures of power dynamics in couples.

Power dynamics in one's family of origin likely shape internalized notions of normative family relationships. Therefore, the division of housework in one's family of origin likely socializes children to hold specific attitudes and beliefs about how relationships should work and how labor is performed in one's own home. We examine this hypothesized relationship in Chapter 9 by examining variation in housework performance and other behaviors, as well as attitudes regarding expectations of heterosexual intimate relationships and parental roles, among young adults based upon the power dynamics and household division of labor that was documented in their homes of origin during their formative years.

Chapter 10 summarizes the key contributions of the book and remarks on the American family of the future. More recent investigations have documented greater similarity in housework time for women and men, but unlike this book, those studies are not based on couple-level data. We conclude by arguing not only for the use of housework as a proxy for power by practitioners, but also for continued investigation into how power dynamics continue to evolve in contemporary American couples.

This book is not meant to construct a typology of housework performance that all couples in the U.S. must fall into. Indeed, we note in Chapter 8 the fluidity of housework performance over time. Instead, this book is meant as a means to understand how we as researchers, practitioners, and others who care about family well-being can use housework as another method of understanding couple dynamics. Housework is easy to talk about, being something that most individuals can relate to. It is our goal that this book provide insights into how we can measure power displays in couples, not only as a scholarly enterprise, but also in order to guide conversations about culturally hidden power that feel less threatening. In that spirit, Chapter 2 introduces the theoretical and empirical literatures that have investigated housework and power.

# Theorizing housework as an example of power dynamics

## Introduction

As described in Chapter 1, theoretical frameworks explaining the division of housework typically fall into two main categories: resource-based and social-psychological/symbolic perspectives. Here, we argue that power can be derived from both material and ideological sources, often simultaneously and in complicated ways. We provide a short summary of two theoretical frameworks categorized as resource-based—time availability and bargaining theory—emphasizing how material resources reflect power when used to avoid performing housework. We follow with a summary of two social-psychological/symbolic theoretical frameworks—gender ideology and economic dependence—and discuss how the performance of housework is connected to the performance of gender beliefs. Each of these perspectives (with the possible exception of the gender ideology perspective) implicitly or explicitly assumes that housework is seen by wives and husbands as something to be avoided and that both wives and husbands attempt to minimize how much housework they do. We conclude the chapter by explaining the process through which housework reflects power dynamics in couples. This argument is the underpinning of the empirical analysis that follows, so we provide examples from empirical research throughout the section in order to help facilitate understanding of the process.

## Time availability perspective

The time availability perspective is most closely associated with human capital theory (for example, Becker, 1981), which argues that households attempt to maximize utility through their members' specialization in either market or non-market labor. This perspective suggests that men have a comparative advantage in market work while women have a comparative advantage in domestic or non-market labor (based largely on their role as mothers). It is also the case that due to men's higher wage rates, the opportunity cost for men to increase their non-market work hours at the expense of market work hours is greater than that for women. Consequently, men's comparative advantage and greater opportunity cost will lead them to concentrate on market work, while women will focus on non-market work due to their comparative advantage and lower opportunity cost in that sphere. As a result, this perspective predicts a strong association between the amount of market work performed and how much housework an individual does. Most studies suggest that employed wives do less housework than wives not in the paid labor market but the differences tend to be small (Arrighi and Maume, 2000).

Bianchi et al (2000) tested specific hypotheses derived from the time availability perspective using data provided by 4,107 couples from Wave 2 of the National Survey of Families and Households collected during 1992–94. They found that wives' market work hours were negatively associated with couples' total housework hours and with their own housework hours, while positively associated with husbands' housework hours. Husbands' hours of market work were negatively associated with their own housework hours and positively associated with wives' housework hours. In other words, the effects of market work on housework performance were consistent with the predictions of the time availability perspective (net of relative resources and gender ideology—for more on those frameworks and their measures, see later).

Sayer's (2005) study expanded upon this line of thinking but added a gender dimension to the conceptualization. Using time-diary data from 1965, 1975, and 1998, she asked "Whether women's and men's time use patterns have become more similar and, if so, why?" (Sayer, 2005: 286). The crux of the argument assessed in her study was that increases in women's wages and educational attainment have reduced their comparative advantage in non-market work, which, according to the time availability perspective, should lead to reallocations in women's time, in particular, to increases in market work and reductions in women's housework time. She found that while women over this time period—in which women were generally increasing their labor-force participation—consistently did more housework and less market work than men, the gender differences had narrowed. Overall, then, there is support for the time availability perspective as an explanation of the division of housework between couples.

## Relative resources or bargaining perspective

Taking an exchange-based view, the relative resources perspective sees the household division of labor as resulting from implicit negotiation between spouses. It assumes that housework is seen as undesirable and that wives and husbands try to avoid doing it. As a result, because wives tend to bring fewer resources (particularly earnings) into the negotiation process, they are less able to produce an outcome favorable to themselves, that is, an equitable division of household labor. This approach suggests that increases in the earning levels and labor-force participation of married women should produce decreases in the amount of household labor by wives. Overall, the spouse with higher earnings should, ceteris paribus, have a stronger bargaining position and (assuming that actors prefer to do as little housework as possible) do less housework. A number of studies confirm this prediction (Greenstein, 2000; Bittman et al, 2003; Evertsson and Nermo 2004). Here, the general finding is that high-earning (relative to their husbands) wives tend to do less housework than low-earning wives. England and Folbre (2005: 640) point out that in Becker's model, "the family has a single utility function and cooperates to allocate each partner's time efficiently," but that in the bargaining model, "partners are not entirely altruistic"—that is, they are not irrevocably bound to a single household utility-maximization scheme—"and where they have a conflict of interest, resources affect whose interests prevail." Several studies have noted that the effects of relative earnings or bargaining position operate differently for women as compared to men (Greenstein, 2000; Atkinson et al, 2005), and have combined the relative earnings arguments with the gender ideology perspective to produce an economic dependence perspective, discussed later.

## Gender ideology perspective

Gender ideologies are how people identify themselves with respect to family and marital roles traditionally linked to gender. Gender ideologies are distinguished from gender identity (Goffman, 1977: 315) in that gender identities are self-definitions, such as male or female, while ideologies are the elements that make up that self-definition. Davis and Greenstein (2009: 89) define "gender ideology" as the "underlying concept of an individual's level of support for a division of paid work and family responsibilities that is based on the notion of separate spheres." These beliefs also implicate issues such as the primacy of the breadwinner role, working women and relationship quality (especially with young children), motherhood and the feminine self, household utility, and the acceptance of male privilege. Bolzendahl and Myers (2004) assert that gender ideologies are the result of both interest-based approaches (individuals are more likely to hold egalitarian or pro-feminist attitudes when their interests are best served by an egalitarian approach) and exposure-based approaches (exposure to situations and individuals supportive of egalitarian ideas leads individuals to hold more egalitarian gender ideologies).

Marriage and other intimate relationships provide arenas in which these ideologies are manifested. Most scholars have assumed that traditional women do more housework than egalitarian women (and traditional men do less housework than egalitarian men), and many previous studies have found this to be the case in single-nation studies from Canada (Brayfield, 1992; Gazso-Windle and McMullin, 2003), China (Pimentel, 2006), Germany (Lavee and Katz, 2002), Great Britain (Baxter, 1992; Kan, 2008), Israel (Lavee and Katz, 2002; Lewin-Epstein et al, 2006), Sweden (Nordenmark and Nyman, 2003), Taiwan (Hu and Kamo, 2007), and the U.S. (Greenstein, 1996a, 1996b; Bianchi et al, 2000; Cunningham, 2005), as well as in cross-national studies (Batalova and Cohen, 2002; Nordenmark, 2004; Davis et al, 2007), to name just a few. Truly, the effect of gender ideology on the division of household labor is robust.

Many studies also suggest that there is an interaction between a woman's gender ideology and that of her male partner in terms of their effects on the division of household labor. Greenstein (1996b) noted that husbands' gender ideology was related to how much domestic work they performed for men married to egalitarian wives but not for men married to traditional wives. He concluded that "husbands do relatively little domestic labor unless both they and their wives are relatively nontraditional in their beliefs about gender and marital roles" (Greenstein, 1996b: 593). Greenstein also suggested that even when it is not the focal independent variable, we need to incorporate gender ideology into our analyses of non-market work, arguing that "It seems unlikely that we can attain a complete understanding of the phenomenon of the division of household labor through purely microeconomic approaches or purely structural approaches" (Greenstein, 1996b: 594).

## Economic dependence perspective

This model posits that housework is women's work because women tend to be economically dependent upon their male partners (for example, Brines, 1994; Greenstein, 2000). This model argues that women and men may perform gender or display gender-deviance neutralization (Bittman et al, 2003), adjusting the amount of housework performed to be consistent with social expectations regarding women's and men's behavior.

This perspective suggests that wives and husbands placed in non-normative roles (breadwinner wives and economically dependent husbands) may compensate for a gender-deviant position by adjusting their housework performance. Breadwinner wives, for example, would be predicted to perform more housework than we would predict from a relative resources perspective, while dependent husbands would do less. A number of studies (Brines, 1994; Greenstein, 2000; Bittman et al., 2003; Thébaud, 2010; Schneider, 2011; Baxter and Hewitt, 2013; Aassve et al, 2014) have found evidence for a gender-deviance neutralization effect.

This particular perspective fell under theoretical scrutiny not long after it was introduced into the literature (Sullivan, 2011). In a review of the literature available at that time, Sullivan (2011: 10) concluded that "considerable doubt is cast on the gender-deviance-neutralization thesis." She presented three main critiques of this line of inquiry. First, she argued that the original research misspecified the analytic models for women by using measures of relative income and not controlling for actual income. However, several studies (for example, Killewald and Gough, 2010; Schneider, 2011) have refuted this criticism and found gender-deviance neutralization effects even when controlling for actual income. Therefore, this specific criticism seems without warrant.

Sullivan's second critique was that the observed effects of gender-deviance neutralization in previous studies were limited to women who were primary breadwinners and to men who were economically dependent, groups that account for very small proportions of their respective gender groups. It is not clear to us why this objection is even relevant to the existence of the phenomenon. The extent to which the effect is widespread is not the issue here; in fact, almost by definition, in patriarchal societies, we would not expect there to be large numbers of breadwinner wives or dependent husbands. Scholars regularly study groups that reflect a proportionately small component of a society; the robust literature on lesbian, gay, bisexual, transgender and queer (LGBTQ) households began as an investigation into a segment of households that was proportionately very small.

Finally, Sullivan (2011: 11) claimed that even if there was a gender-deviance neutralization effect among economically dependent husbands in the 1980s and 1990s, "recent changes in both attitudes and practice among men have meant that it is probably no longer a significant phenomenon." However, the fact that studies using data gathered after 2000 (for example, Thébaud, 2010; Schneider, 2012; Aassve et al, 2014) that have found evidence of an effect among husbands continue to appear in print suggests otherwise. Moreover, there are numerous studies published after Sullivan's (2011) paper that have reported gender-deviance neutralization effects (for example, Usdansky and Parker, 2011; Baxter and Hewitt, 2013; Bertrand et al, 2013; Kolpashnikova, 2018). Overall, then, this particular perspective, with its explicit inclusion of how household behaviors, gender, and power are interconnected, remains salient and important in the study of housework.

## Previous discussions of power in relationships

Outlining the process of change in families with a focus on the gendered division of household labor, Sullivan (2006) provides a good synopsis of research on marital power, as well as a nuanced, integrated framework for thinking about housework overall. She highlights the importance of embedded interactions as the nexus of change in gendered relationships, especially those around the division of housework. Embedded interactions are the "interaction and negotiation that takes place in specific contexts of gender consciousness, relational and material resources, and the wider discursive environment..... It refers to the dynamic processes of the daily interaction between partners, embedded within their social and discursive context" (Sullivan, 2006: 108, 109–10). In Sullivan's (2006) framework, these interactions have a recursive relationship with different types of resources that can be called upon to use in the daily interaction: structural or material resources (usually operationalized as [women's] employment status, absolute and relative income, and educational resources); and relational resources (influences promoting reflexivity and self-awareness in intimate relationships, usually indicated by exposure to therapeutic culture or self-help discourse [Benjamin and Sullivan, 1996, 1999]).

Revisiting Emerson's (1962, 1972a, 1972b) theory on power-dependence relations in this context of understanding marital power is a useful endeavor. One of the key points in his work is that there is a need to clarify conceptual ambiguity around the notions of "power," "authority," "legitimacy," and "influence," among others. Emerson (1962: 32) argues that "power resides implicitly in the other's dependency"; in other words, the power that a person holds over another person resides in the control over the things that the other values. This set of relations is in a relationship where the actors are mutually dependent on one another—and an intimate relationship like a marriage certainly fits this description. Emerson (1962: 32) defines power as "the amount of resistance on the part of [actor] B which can be potentially overcome by [actor] A." This only works as a definition if A makes a demand and if that demand is something that B is not likely to do willingly.

Forty years after Emerson's original work, Tichenor (2005) wrote about conceptualizing power within marriage. Her perspective on power is considerably more nuanced than Emerson's, introducing the concepts of "overt" and "latent" power. **Overt power**—how much say a person has—is the ability to control or influence decision-making. Tichenor argues that the actual outcome of the decision-making is less important to understanding overt power in a relationship than is the actual process of negotiation (or lack thereof). **Latent power** is the ability to suppress issues through the successful resolution of issues in the past to prevent their being brought up again.

Tichenor also reminds us of Lukes's (2005) concept of **hidden power**, which is the ability to keep particular issues from entering the arena of conflict. Further, institutional arrangements and prevailing ideological constructions may make any individual's or group's domination seem natural; thus, the ability of one person to influence another—the use of power—is hidden. As Tichenor notes, hidden power is

> exercised through individual decisions, institutional procedures, and dominant values that shape interaction.... [T]he concept of hidden power is useful as it allows us to assess how cultural expectations regarding gender at the institutional level affect both the interactions between spouses and their attempts to construct meaningful identities. Attention to hidden power can sensitize us to the subtle ways in which gender expectations shape the power dynamics within marriage. (2005: 26)

For example, Zipp, Prohaska, and Bemiller's (2004) research on the extent to which spouses' knowledge of their partner's survey response led to increased similarity in the survey answers provides evidence of men's hidden power in marriages. Zipp et al found that, contrary to expectations from structural equivalence theory (where husbands' responses would be more similar to their wives' in areas where women typically have expertise [household-related issues] and wives' responses would be more similar to their husbands' in areas where men typically have expertise [political issues]), women were more affected by their husbands' responses on political issues than men were when they heard their wives' responses overall. Zipp et al examined whether these patterns held when men held less traditional power in their relationship than their wives or held markers of not being the senior partner (for example, educational attainment, household income, and employment status) and found that those men were not significantly more likely to have survey responses similar to their wives as compared to men who occupied the traditional role of head of household. Thus, Zipp et al found evidence of men's hidden power influencing their wives' reported attitudes.

If we combine Emerson's (1962) definition of power with the concepts of overt, latent, and hidden power, we can frame housework as something that people are unwilling to do and that is under the purview of one actor who then has to figure out, perhaps through the use of power, how to get another actor to participate. Culturally, housework (including the mental work of making sure that all household tasks are performed [Daly, [2002]) is women's work, so research has traditionally tried to understand how women in heterosexual relationships (typically marriages, so the frame of mutual dependency is maintained) get men to do work that they would not willingly do. Blood and Wolfe's (1960) work connects back to the resources that each partner has that they may make available to the other partner in order to help them. Again, they focus on power as evidenced in decision-making (like financial decisions, career prioritization and timing, and so on). They argue that power is "a mutual recognition of individual skills in particular areas of competence and of the partner's dual stake in areas of joint concerns" (Blood and Wolfe, 1960: 45). Blood and Wolfe also note that housework does not have to be done by women (but it largely was at the time of their writing as a function of time availability), and although men have a moral obligation to help when needed, couples largely specialize. Their book was written at a specific point in American history (in 1960) but we can try to connect their ideas of power and housework in marriage with Emerson's (1962) discussion of power broadly to think through how we have and have not been assessing marital power in our research on housework in ways consonant with these classic treatises.

One of Emerson's most important theoretical contributions was his argument that power is a property of social relations, not of social actors. Consequently, a key issue in thinking about the operationalization of power in the literature on the division of household labor is the identification of the location of the power and where it resides. If power is an attribute of relationships rather than of specific actors in the relationship, then the ways in which we have typically operationalized power in our quantitative research need to be re-examined if we believe that, as a contested site, housework can be a mechanism through which power may be illuminated. By measuring power as primarily a tangible possession, as social scientists typically do with resources like income, education, or knowledge, we have attributed power to social actors and removed it from being a property of the relationship itself. However, there is nothing in Emerson's perspective on power (or, indeed, in most exchange-based formulations) that limits us to analyses of exchanges involving tangible commodities. Indeed, the most interesting cases arise over the study of the most fundamental intangible or symbolic commodities: love, affection, and respect. By expanding our analyses of power and exchange to include symbolic commodities, we are better able to take the context of the social relationship into consideration.

Housework has historically been defined as women's work, with the exception of a few discretionary activities like lawn care and maintenance activities that are largely the responsibility of men (for a discussion of the gendered nature of core and non-core tasks, see Bianchi et al, 2000). When a woman and a man form a union (marital or otherwise), regardless of what types of labor they performed in their previous households, the path of least resistance, that status quo (to use Kluwer's [2011] language), is for women to do the majority of tasks and spend more time than do men on housework. Power is then evidenced when women are able to do less than would be expected in these circumstances. Resources that are usually seen as those representing the possibility of giving the partner something are specific to the cultural and historic times, namely, money and, to a lesser extent, education and occupational prestige. Theoretical perspectives focus on women's relative resources and economic dependency as measures of their power relative to their husbands. What is interesting, then, is the new debate over the influence of women's absolute income on housework time (for example, Gupta, 2006, 2007; Gupta and Ash, 2008) as it requires us to take into consideration that couples where women are relatively more powerful, as captured by the education, income, and occupation measures, tend to be unique and/or short-lived. Thus, the power-dependence models that focus on these structural/material resources really only explain men's behavior. Power is gendered, at least in the context of intimate/married relationships.

As noted earlier, Blood and Wolfe proposed the resource/exchange model: resources such as income and status represent the potential for exercising power. Men had more power because they had more resources, not because of patriarchal ideology. Later research found that when women have these resources, they are not able to activate power to the same extent that men are; this has to mean that power is also about gender. For example, Tichenor's research highlights the empirical reality that resources do not equal power. She writes that

> women's incomes have bought them little in their marriage because the gender structure assures men certain privileges within the marital relationship ... couples with higher earning wives present a more serious challenge to the gender structure.... couples' efforts to preserve men's authority and interpersonal dominance ... highlight the difficulty of rewriting conventional gender scripts and demonstrate the resilience of the gender structure. (2005: 23)

As with other behaviors, housework produces gender (Berk, 1985; West and Zimmerman, 1987). That is, the performance of household tasks produces and reproduces culturally expected relationships between individuals that are tied both to masculinity and femininity and to the power inherent in the relationship between masculine and feminine. The performance (or lack of performance) of housework can be seen as reaffirming an individual's sense of self as a masculine or feminine person (Brines, 1994; Greenstein, 2000; Killewald, 2011; Sullivan, 2011; Tichenor, 2005), and, in particular, as a husband or a wife. Previous research has demonstrated the ways in which housework is used and is believed to be used to produce gender (Hochschild and Machung, 1989; DeVault, 1990). While husbands and wives may choose to perform certain tasks like cooking or yard maintenance because they enjoy them, as individuals, they are held morally accountable to standards associated with their presumed sex category. Further, the tasks themselves are gendered, so when there is praise or scrutiny applied to the performance of a task, it will likely automatically be given to the person who was expected to have performed the task.

The difficulty in changing gendered expectations has been documented by many authors, some querying whether we can "undo" gender as we know it (Lorber, 2005; Risman, 2009; West and Zimmerman, 2009). Indeed, the primacy of gender as a set of relationships within a culture becomes more clear once changes in other markers of power in the performance of work in a culture (such as income) are seen to lead to minimal changes in the division of housework (see, for example, Brines, 1994; Greenstein, 2000; Tichenor, 2005). Although, as noted earlier, Sullivan (2011) argues that the evidence for gender-deviance neutralization (where individuals performing tasks inappropriate for their gender compensate in other ways, like unemployed men performing less housework than employed men so as not to be seen as feminine) is relatively weak, we cannot ignore inequality in the division of household labor when both spouses are equal participants in the market or hold similar markers of power like education and income. Inequality in housework in this circumstance can be seen as evidence of the primacy of cultural gender norms in marriages.

So, how can we use this discussion to help us understand power more generally? Emerson (1962) also argued that social scientists should look at the interaction process to locate factors leading to perceived power and dependency, as well as the conditions under which power in its potential form would actually be employed. For example, Pesquera (1993) documents some of the conditions under which change in household labor can occur. One condition, beyond structural/conventional issues of marital power, is women's level of comfort in negotiation around the division of housework with their husbands. The combination of direct and indirect approaches is tied to women's willingness to engage in what Pesquera terms a political struggle over the performance of housework. Women who not only wanted to do less housework, but also *believed* that their husbands *should* do more, were more likely to directly request their husbands' participation and to use "underground" tactics to get their husbands to do more. This political struggle was the result of women's beliefs regarding housework and was evidence of their own marital power (Pesquera, 1993).

## Summary

Explaining the division of housework in couples has historically drawn upon logics that either directly or indirectly invoke power dynamics. For example, a spouse who has more absolute or relative material power (or both), as measured by income or education, has been theorized to be able to negotiate their way out of performing housework, and the literature outlined earlier documents support for that explanation. Individuals who believe that there is a gendered component to the division of paid and unpaid work not only attempt to enact that gendered division of labor through their own performance of housework, but may also either coerce their spouse (using power) or be coerced (acquiescing to power) into enacting that division of labor. Research has supported that perspective as well.

What has not been examined is the extent to which housework can be seen as a reflection of the total power dynamic in a couple. The literature has typically focused on one power dynamic at a time, or when examining measures of power simultaneously, has not been able to provide a holistic view of a couple's division of labor. We argue that a couple's division of housework reflects how power is simultaneously enacted and reinforced within the household. We argue that the political struggle over housework as described by Pesquera (1993) reflects hidden power (Zipp et al, 2004) embodied in material and symbolic resources. Therefore, modeling a couple's division of labor as a social process—one that is negotiated through the use of (and response to) hidden power—should allow us to see how power operates within a couple. Before moving into Chapter 4, where we perform such an analysis using couple-level data to construct a typology of couples based upon their division of housework, Chapter 3 sets the social and historical context for the families whose experiences are analyzed in this book.

# 3

# Describing the data

## Introduction

Our investigations into demonstrating the extent to which housework can be considered a proxy for couples' power relationships led us to use data from the three waves of the National Survey of Families and Households (NSFH) (see Sweet et al, 1988) gathered in 1987/88, 1992/94, and 2001/03. These data are particularly useful for our purposes since they represent one of the very few national probability surveys that interviewed both members of couples (as well as their adult children). The NSFH is a national probability sample of 13,008 households, including oversamples of black people, Puerto Ricans, Mexican-Americans, single-parent families, families with stepchildren, cohabiting couples, and recently married persons. There were a total of 7,215 married-couple households and 710 cohabiting-couple households at Wave 1 of the NSFH. We limited our analyses to heterosexual couples; our analyses required that we have complete household labor data on both the primary respondent and the primary respondent's spouse/partner, yielding a working sample of 3,906 couples at Wave 1. These 3,906 couples form the basis for all of our subsequent analyses.

It will be obvious to the reader that the Wave 1 data under study here are more than 30 years old as of the time of this book's publication. While this is problematic if the purpose of the research is to make generalizations about the exact housework behavior of contemporary couples, that is not our goal. Rather, we are using these data to investigate whether and how the distribution of housework between wives and their husbands can be seen as an indicator or proxy for power in their relationships. In other words, our concern with the empirical evidence is more theoretical and conceptual than it is descriptive. While the exact parameters of housework have undoubtedly changed over the last 30 years, we believe that the conceptual and theoretical connections between housework and power within couples have not, making our empirical investigation relevant for both contemporary and future social-scientific discussions about families and households.

## Situating the NSFH data in social and historical context

Given the age of the data, it is wise to consider the social and historical context within which the NSFH couples were living their lives in the late 1980s in order to understand the social-structural constraints and opportunities available to the couples culturally. The period saw an economic recession followed by a period of sustained economic growth. In the U.S., "Reaganomics" yielded an emphasis on the reduction of taxes and a general promotion of free markets. Reaganomics assumed that tax reductions would stimulate increased investment and job creation. Such policies in the U.S. were mirrored by Margaret Thatcher's Conservative government in the U.K. Following a long period of economic growth, the early 1990s were characterized by a mild recession often attributed to the restrictive monetary policies of Reagan and his successor, George H.W. Bush. The 1990/91 recession saw U.S. unemployment rates peak at 7.8 percent and job losses of more than 1.5 million.

On the demographic front, divorce rates in the U.S. peaked around 1980, then started a decline that has continued through the present day. Long-term decreases in fertility rates following the end of the "Baby Boom" continued. There were dramatic increases in women's labor-force participation, especially among women with young children. Ages at first marriage continued to climb for both men and women, and by the end of the decade, only about half of all households in the U.S. were headed by married couples. There were marked increases in "non-traditional" households, such as single-parent households and households composed of cohabiting couples and single persons living alone.

Turning to social issues, evangelical and fundamentalist groups grew in number and visibility. Outspoken conservatives such as Phyllis Schlafly led the growing criticism of feminism and opposition to abortion rights. Much of the discussion concerning families centered around what came to be known as "family values" (a panchreston that could mean anything to anyone) as the focus began to shift back from the liberal idea that the state and society should support the family to the conservative approach that families should support society. Conservatives ushered in the beginning of responses to what they called the "War on the Family," suggesting that "non-traditional" family forms such as single parents, cohabiting couples, and same-sex couples represented an existential threat to the "traditional" family, which they viewed as a married heterosexual couple headed by a breadwinning father and a homemaker wife.

## Describing the housework data

Given the social chaos of the late 1980s and early 1990s, it is not surprising to find great diversity in the way in which American couples in the NSFH organized their lives, including their distribution of housework. In this chapter, we provide general background information on the performance of housework by the couples in our analytic sample. Table 3.1 shows the average number of hours per week spent by wives and their husbands on each of nine housework tasks: meal preparation, kitchen clean-up and dishwashing, general housecleaning, yardwork, grocery shopping, laundry, paying bills, car maintenance, and driving family members.

The most obvious conclusion from Table 3.1 is that women did far more housework than men: on average, women performed about twice as many hours of housework per week as their male partners. It is also important to note that the kinds of tasks that women and men did were highly gendered. Women did roughly four times as much meal preparation, kitchen work, general cleaning, and laundry work as did men. Men's hours exceeded those of their partners only for two tasks: yardwork and car maintenance. For the remaining three tasks (grocery shopping, paying bills, and driving family members), women held a slight edge.

Table 3.1: Mean number of hours per week spent on household tasks by wives and husbands

|  | Wives | Husbands |
| --- | --- | --- |
| Meal preparation | 9.86 (7.09) | 2.68 (3.89) |
| Kitchen | 8.05 (6.64) | 2.50 (3.90) |
| General cleaning | 8.36 (8.01) | 2.03 (3.54) |
| Yardwork | 2.02 (4.25) | 5.30 (6.54) |
| Grocery shopping | 2.94 (3.00) | 1.60 (2.18) |
| Laundry | 4.41 (4.29) | 0.76 (2.05) |
| Paying bills | 1.76 (2.84) | 1.44 (2.71) |
| Car maintenance | 0.23 (1.49) | 1.92 (3.52) |
| Driving family members | 1.51 (3.22) | 1.29 (3.35) |
| All household tasks | 38.36 (22.26) | 19.16 (15.90) |

Notes: $N$ = 3,906 couples. Table entries are mean hours per week with standard deviations in parentheses.

## Housework distributions and demographic characteristics

The remaining tables in this chapter examine differences in housework performance by gender and eight background or demographic characteristics: union status, race, educational attainment, age, couple income, metropolitan status, geographical region, and religious affiliation. Due to the substantial differences in housework performance by gender noted earlier, all of the tables report results separately for women and for men.

Table 3.2 compares the distribution of housework for married couples and cohabiting couples. Here, and consistent with similar studies published using more recent data (for example, Davis et al, 2007), we find that men in cohabiting relationships did more housework than married men, while married women did more housework than cohabiting women. Married women performed about 7.25 hours per week more housework than cohabiting women; cohabiting men did about two hours more per week than married men.

With regard to race, in Table 3.3, we find that white women and Hispanic women did more than twice as many hours of household labor as their male partners. However, while black men and men of other races were somewhat closer to parity with their female partners, the gap was still substantial. We also note that among women, Hispanics did the most housework by a considerable margin, while black men did substantially more housework than men of other races.

**Table 3.2:** Mean number of hours per week spent on household tasks by union status

|  | Wives | Husbands |
| --- | --- | --- |
| Currently married | 39.02 (22.15) | 18.98 (15.74) |
| Currently cohabiting | 31.73 (22.26) | 20.98 (17.41) |

Notes: N = 3,906 couples. Table entries are mean hours per week with standard deviations in parentheses.

**Table 3.3:** Mean number of hours per week spent on household tasks by race

|  | Wives | Husbands |
| --- | --- | --- |
| White, non-Hispanic | 38.19 (22.08) | 18.61 (14.81) |
| Black | 39.12 (22.82) | 23.64 (21.88) |
| Hispanic | 42.38 (24.83) | 19.92 (18.35) |
| Other, not specified | 31.74 (17.86) | 19.95 (17.95) |

Notes: N = 3,906 couples. Table entries are mean hours per week with standard deviations in parentheses.

For women, there was a clear negative relationship between highest degree earned and how much housework they do. Table 3.4 shows that the range is impressive, from 43.54 hours per week for women who did not finish high school to just under 31 hours for women with a graduate or professional degree. No such relationship is apparent for men. In all educational groups, though, women did far more housework than their male partners.

Table 3.5 shows the relationship between economic status and housework. Here, there was a negative association between couple income and number of hours of housework performed per week for both women and men. Some of this effect is undoubtedly due to couples purchasing goods and services—for example, house-cleaning services, takeout meals, yardwork, and so on—in the market. In all four groups, women still did about twice as much housework as their partners.

There are sizable differences in housework performed by women and men in metropolitan as opposed to non-metropolitan areas. Table 3.6 shows that while women in metropolitan areas did six fewer hours of housework per week than those in non-metropolitan areas, men

**Table 3.4**: Mean number of hours per week spent on household tasks by educational attainment

|  | Wives | Husbands |
|---|---|---|
| Less than high school degree | 43.54 (25.39) | 18.91 (18.80) |
| High school degree | 41.42 (22.86) | 19.74 (16.73) |
| Some college, associate degree | 36.01 (20.38) | 20.75 (16.15) |
| Bachelor's degree | 32.53 (19.02) | 17.28 (11.98) |
| Graduate/professional degree | 30.99 (17.95) | 17.52 (11.89) |

Notes: $N$ = 3,906 couples. Table entries are mean hours per week with standard deviations in parentheses.

**Table 3.5**: Mean number of hours per week spent on household tasks by household income quartile

|  | Wives | Husbands |
|---|---|---|
| Lowest income quartile | 41.82 (24.63) | 20.89 (18.89) |
| Second income quartile | 40.00 (22.84) | 19.99 (16.78) |
| Third income quartile | 37.62 (20.39) | 19.48 (15.09) |
| Highest income quartile | 33.97 (20.26) | 17.30 (12.58) |

Notes: $N$ = 3,312 couples. Table entries are mean hours per week with standard deviations in parentheses.

**Table 3.6:** Mean number of hours per week spent on household tasks by metropolitan status

|  | Wives | Husbands |
|---|---|---|
| In metropolitan area | 36.87 (21.51) | 19.25 (15.58) |
| Not in metropolitan area | 42.47 (23.73) | 18.90 (16.74) |

Notes: N = 3,906 couples. Table entries are mean hours per week with standard deviations in parentheses.

living in metropolitan areas did more housework than men living in non-metropolitan areas.

Table 3.7 shows differences in the performance of housework across geographical regions in the U.S. Both women and their male partners did the least housework in the Northeast region, while women and men in the West region did the most housework. Again, the roughly two-to-one ratio of women's housework hours to men's was consistent across regions.

The most interesting finding in Table 3.8 is that in the late 1980s, younger couples seemed to be approaching gender equity more so than older couples. For women and men aged 18 to 29, the ratio of women's housework hours to men's was about 1.75 to 1; for all of the older groups, it was 2 to 1 or greater. Furthermore, whereas the oldest group (65 years and older) did the most housework among women,

**Table 3.7:** Mean number of hours per week spent on household tasks by region of U.S.

|  | Wives | Husbands |
|---|---|---|
| Northeast | 36.60 (21.05) | 18.14 (14.85) |
| North Central | 38.34 (22.60) | 19.26 (15.45) |
| South | 38.83 (21.78) | 19.04 (17.09) |
| West | 39.30 (23.62) | 20.22 (15.32) |

Notes: N = 3,906 couples. Table entries are mean hours per week with standard deviations in parentheses.

**Table 3.8:** Mean number of hours per week spent on household tasks by age

|  | Wives | Husbands |
|---|---|---|
| 18–29 years | 37.59 (22.63) | 21.43 (18.00) |
| 30–39 years | 38.92 (21.76) | 18.85 (14.18) |
| 40–49 years | 37.85 (21.98) | 18.12 (15.04) |
| 50–64 years | 38.41 (21.96) | 17.75 (15.40) |
| 65 years and older | 40.18 (23.29) | 19.07 (17.73) |

Notes: N = 3,906 couples. Table entries are mean hours per week with standard deviations in parentheses.

among men, it was the opposite: men aged 18–29 years did upwards of two hours of housework per week more than the second highest group (men aged 65 years and older).

Finally, in Table 3.9, we look at housework differences by religious affiliation. Among women, Jews and those of other faiths did the most housework—over 39 hours per week—while those professing no faith did the least (34.08 hours per week). Jewish men did the least housework (14.77 hours per week) while Protestant men did the most (20.19 hours per week). Of course, this gross categorization of religious affiliation almost certainly masks substantial variation within the categories.

**Table 3.9:** Mean number of hours per week spent on household tasks by religious affiliation

|  | Wives | Husbands |
| --- | --- | --- |
| No religious affiliation | 34.08 (20.35) | 19.76 (15.62) |
| Roman Catholic | 38.78 (22.98) | 18.84 (15.40) |
| Jewish | 39.60 (22.28) | 14.77 (10.25) |
| Protestant | 38.85 (22.17) | 20.19 (18.23) |
| Other | 39.69 (23.54) | 18.74 (14.17) |

Notes: $N$ = 3,862 couples (no religion data for $N$ = 39 wives and $N$ = 43 husbands). Table entries are mean hours per week with standard deviations in parentheses.

## Summary

The nine tables in this chapter paint an intriguing picture of variations in the performance of routine household tasks by American couples in the late 1980s. The overall pattern presented by these analyses is that of great diversity and inequality in the division of household labor. Most importantly, we notice that gender was by far the best single predictor of how much housework a person did. On average, women did twice as many hours of housework per week as did men. Not only did women do far more housework than men, but the types of household labor that women and men performed were also gendered. Women did most of the cooking, cleaning, kitchen work, and laundry, while men did most of the yardwork and car maintenance.

We also note systematic relationships between housework performance and social class. Educational attainment was negatively associated with the amount of housework performed for women, but positively associated for men. On the other hand, income was negatively associated with housework performance for both women and men. There are also substantial differences in the division of household labor by race, metropolitan status, region, age, religious affiliation, and whether a couple is married or cohabiting. In short, nearly every personal or social indicator that we study is related to who does how much housework.

Given these wide variations in housework performance across social categories, it should not surprise us to find that there are distinct patterns of housework allocation among U.S. couples. In Chapter 4, we will use these NSFH data to model these patterns and use them to aid us in showing how housework can be considered a proxy for power in couple relationships.

# 4

# The five classes

## Introduction

As we argued in Chapters 1 and 2, housework can be seen as a proxy for power relations in a couple. We start from the assumption that partners prefer not to do housework and that they will take steps to minimize the amount of housework they do. Partners negotiate the performance of tasks across time in their relationships through the mechanisms of social exchange and construct, however fleeting, a normative distribution of tasks that reflects their ability to escape the performance of tasks that they would prefer not to perform. Layered within this normative distribution of tasks within each couple are their own understandings of gender display as gender and power are inextricably linked. Therefore, constructing a typology of the division of housework would necessarily require an investigation of power derived from both material and cultural origins.

## Constructing the classes

Our investigations into demonstrating the extent to which housework can be considered a proxy for power relationships in a couple led us to construct an empirically based typology of American heterosexual couples. With data from the first wave of the National Survey of Families and Households (NSFH) (see Sweet et al, 1988) gathered in 1987/88 (for a description of the NSFH data, see Chapter 3), we used latent profile analysis (LPA) to classify these 3,906 couples into five general classifications, or classes (for methodological details on LPA, see the Appendix).

These five classes were determined by examining the average amount of time that the wife and husband each spent on nine housework tasks: meal preparation, kitchen work, cleaning, grocery shopping, doing laundry, paying bills, performing yard work, performing car maintenance, and driving for the household. The patterns that emerged from the LPA reflect five classes that describe how the couples divide their time across housework tasks. We labeled the classes "Ultra-Traditional," "Traditional," "Transitional Husbands,"

"Egalitarian," and "Egalitarian High Workload" based upon how the spouses divided their labor, both within the couples and regarding the amount of overall time they spent on the tasks. Figure 4.1 displays the overall patterns of the division of housework tasks by all five classes simultaneously; the data are taken from Table A2 in the Appendix. For ease of presentation, we have categorized housework as traditionally feminine tasks, neutral tasks, and traditionally masculine tasks in a manner consistent with previous literature (Twiggs et al, 1999; Coltrane, 2000).

Both Ultra-Traditional and Traditional couples divided housework by gender, with wives spending more time on traditionally feminine tasks (meal preparation, kitchen work, cleaning, and laundry) while husbands spent more time on traditionally masculine tasks (yard work and car maintenance). The difference in the two types of couples was that the amount of time that wives spent on their tasks was approximately double that of husbands and the time that husbands spent on yard work in particular was significantly higher in Ultra-Traditional couples. Similarly, Egalitarian and Egalitarian High Workload couples reported similar amounts of time across tasks for both husbands and wives, with Egalitarian High Workload couples performing more labor overall as a couple. Couples classified as Transitional Husbands reported labor time on tasks for wives similar to both Traditional and Egalitarian couples but the labor time on traditionally female tasks among the husbands was higher than that for traditional couples.

In the next sections, we provide more in-depth information about each of the classes. We first describe housework time by general categories and follow with details regarding specific tasks as performed by both wives and husbands.

## Ultra-Traditional couples

Ultra-Traditional couples are characterized by a highly gendered division of housework tasks, with wives shouldering an enormous burden of time on traditionally feminine tasks, as shown in Figure 4.2. Differences between wives and their husbands are particularly large for the traditionally feminine tasks such as meal preparation, kitchen work, and cleaning, on which wives spend an average of 47 hours per week compared to their husbands' 3.4 hours, as documented in Figure 4.3. However, Ultra-Traditional wives also spent the most time on masculine tasks of any of the classes (see Table A2 in the Appendix).

**Figure 4.1:** Housework distribution across all classes

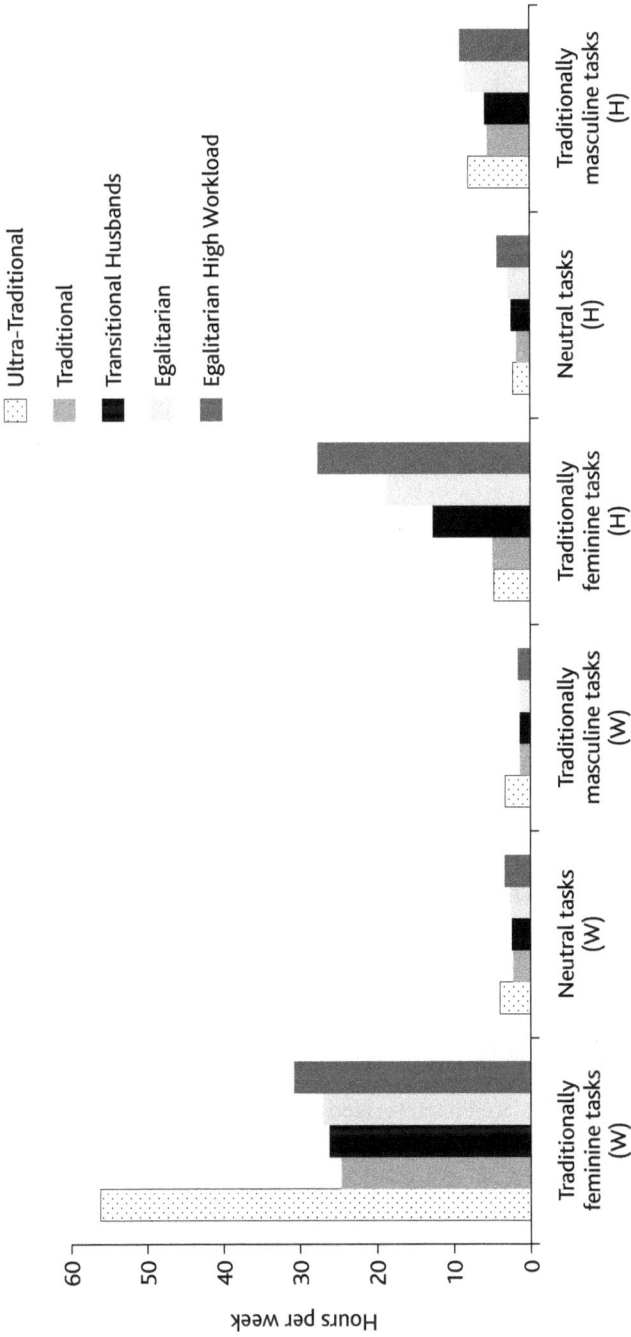

**Figure 4.2**: Ultra-Traditional couples' summary housework distribution

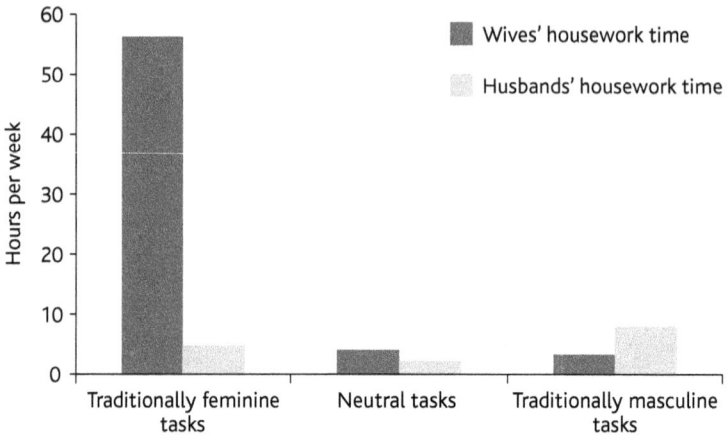

**Figure 4.3**: Ultra-Traditional couples' housework distribution

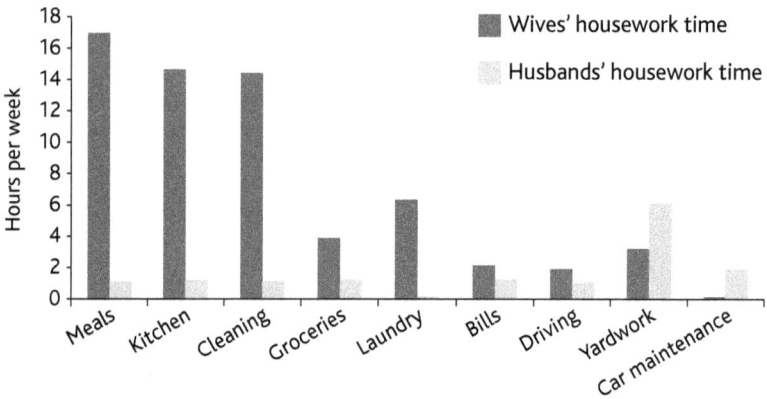

## Traditional couples

These couples are characterized by much less overall housework being performed by both wives and their husbands (see Figure 4.4). They perform a total of about 40 hours per week, about half of what the Ultra-Traditional couples do, even though there are still substantial differences between wives and their husbands, particularly on feminine tasks, as noted in Figure 4.5. Although they do far less total housework, the distributions look very similar to those of the Ultra-Traditional couples. On a side note, the Traditional couples comprise the largest portion of the sample (52.6 percent).

**Figure 4.4:** Traditional couples' summary housework distribution

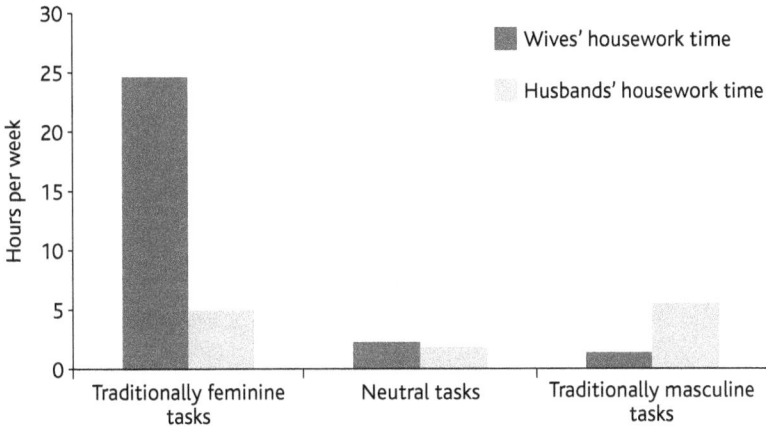

**Figure 4.5:** Traditional couples' housework distribution

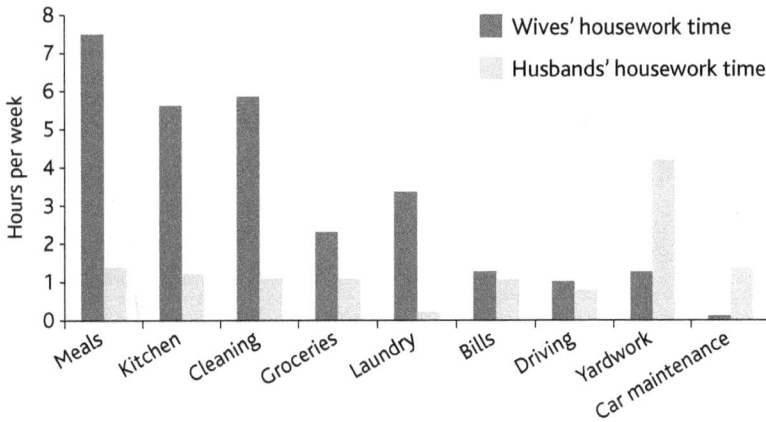

## Transitional Husbands couples

These couples show more participation in housework by husbands (an average of 21 hours per week compared to 30 hours for their wives) and much smaller differences on feminine tasks than either of the traditional groups (see Figures 4.6 and 4.7). We labeled this group "Transitional Husbands" as the husbands' behavior reflected a transitional stage between the two traditional and two egalitarian groups. Their participation in housework—for both wives and husbands—is generally in the middle of the distributions for the entire sample.

**Figure 4.6:** Transitional Husbands couples' summary housework distribution

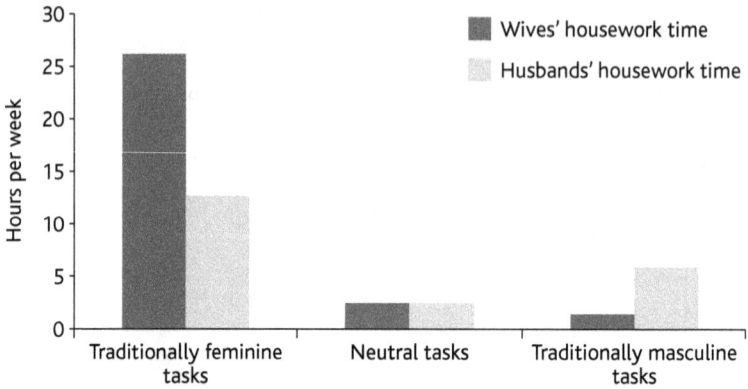

**Figure 4.7:** Transitional Husbands couples' housework distribution

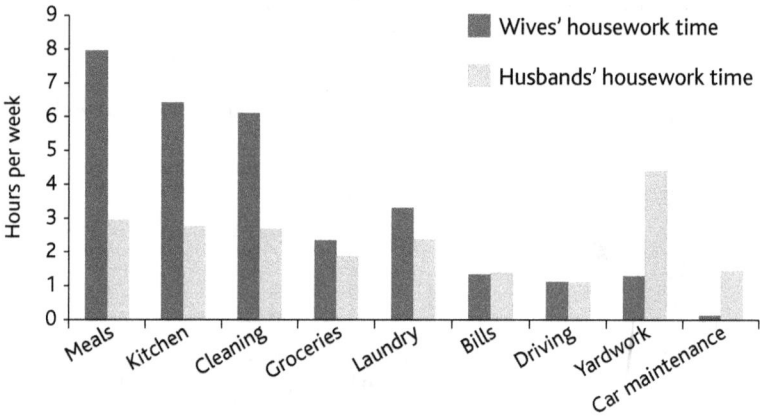

## Egalitarian couples

Egalitarian couples very nearly split the housework burden equally (31 hours for wives; 30 hours for husbands), with much less differentiation on the feminine tasks than the three preceding groups, as noted in Figure 4.8. However, even among these more egalitarian couples, husbands continue to perform substantially more of the masculine tasks, especially yardwork, than do wives (see Figure 4.9). Within the sample, their distributions are most similar to the Egalitarian High Workload couples, described next.

**Figure 4.8**: Egalitarian couples' summary housework distribution

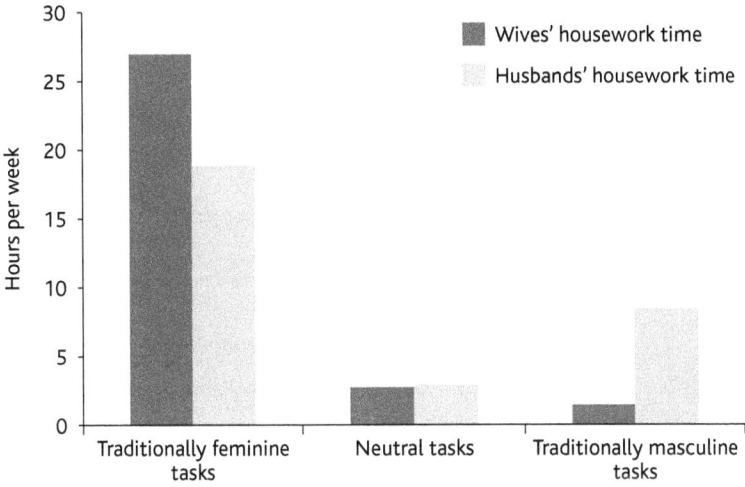

**Figure 4.9**: Egalitarian couples' housework distribution

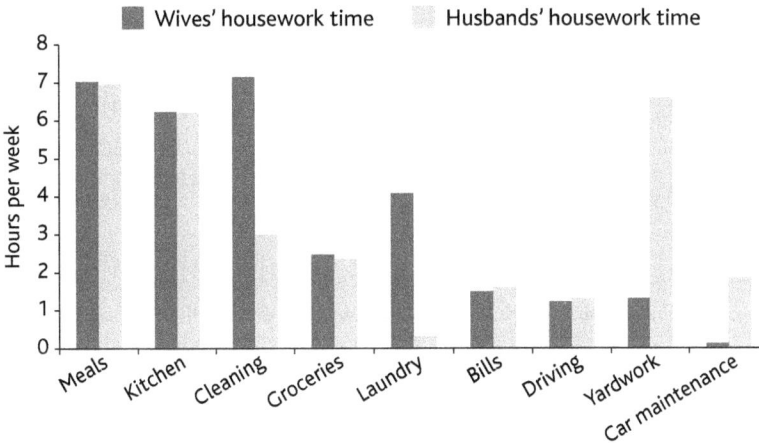

## Egalitarian High Workload couples

Egalitarian High Workload couples comprise the smallest of our five groups (about 4.6 percent of our nearly four thousand couples). Compared to the other four groups, the Egalitarian High Workload couples are quite anomalous. This is the only group where husbands report doing more housework than their wives (41 hours compared to 35 hours per week). Husbands and wives spend almost the same amount of time on feminine tasks (about 24 hours per week for wives and 22 hours per week for husbands), as shown in Figure 4.10. In fact, Egalitarian High Workload husbands do more hours of feminine tasks—almost 31 hours per week—than any of the other classes (see Table A2 in the Appendix). However, as noted in Figure 4.11, husbands continue to outperform wives on masculine tasks such as yardwork and car maintenance.

**Figure 4.10:** Egalitarian High Workload couples' summary housework distribution

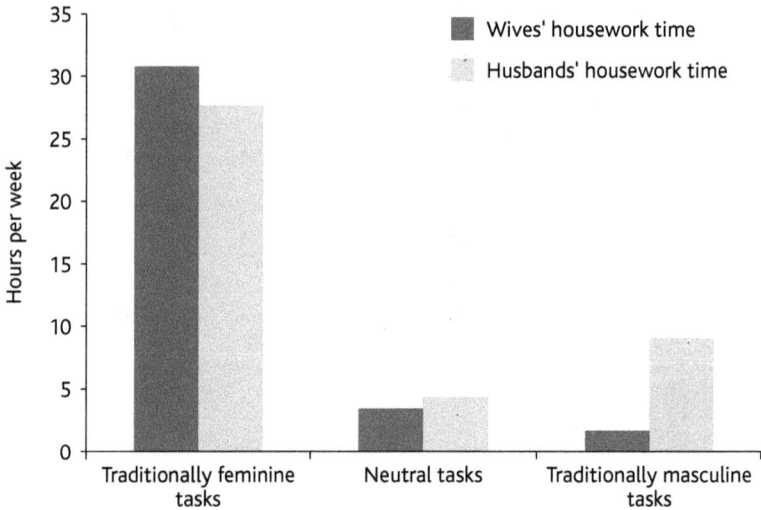

**Figure 4.11:** Egalitarian High Workload couples' housework distribution

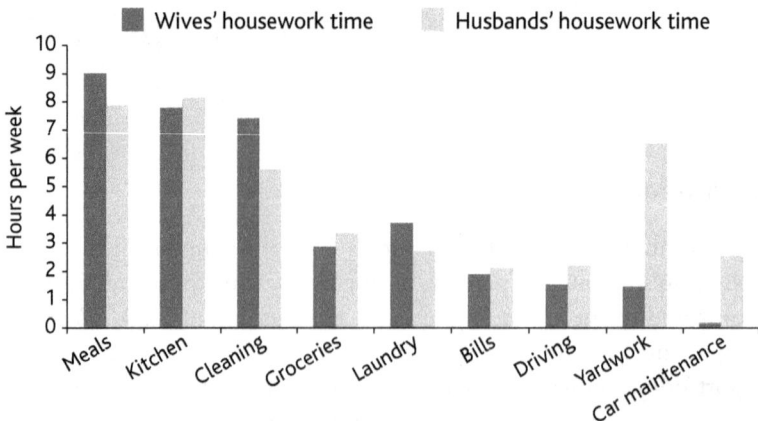

## Summary

The five classes of couples—Ultra-Traditional, Traditional, Transitional Husbands, Egalitarian, and Egalitarian High Workload—reflect five patterns of the distribution of nine household labor tasks between husbands and wives. Upon initial inspection, the classes seem to reflect gender-based power dynamics in the couples, just as we theorized in Chapter 2. Ultra-Traditional couples reflect men's ability to shun housework tasks, especially those tasks typically thought of as feminine; Traditional couples reflect this power dynamic as well, but to a lesser extent. Those in the Transitional Husbands class have a division of labor that reflects men's differential willingness to perform housework, potentially reflecting either women's increased latent power or men's increased willingness to engage in household labor. It should also be noted that the classes where husbands perform the most yardwork (a traditionally masculine task) are those classes where women and men are most likely to share housework tasks in general. The two more egalitarian classes reflect men's increased likelihood of performing traditionally feminine tasks.

The classes that resulted from the LPA analyses reflect gendered dynamics being enacted in couples. Men are able to eschew housework in some couples but are actively engaged in the performance of housework in others. While women continue to perform the bulk of housework hours, regardless of task type, when men do engage in work, it follows two patterns. First, they perform masculine tasks when they begin to engage. Consistent with the literature (Blair and Lichter, 1991; Coltrane and Ishii-Kuntz, 1992), men's housework hours increased in yardwork and car maintenance first. However, also consistent with the literature, when men performed feminine tasks, it was cooking rather than cleaning that was performed. This behavior is consistent with the changing gender norms of the time (Hochschild and Machung, 1989; Twiggs et al, 1999). Second, when men performed very high levels of housework, so did women. This is evident in the two egalitarian classes but especially among the Egalitarian High Workload couples.

The patterns of housework performance across the couples in our sample are consistent with qualitative research performed around the time that the data were collected. Hochschild and Machung (1989) were among the first authors to use the language of "transitional" to describe individuals (but most often men) whose attitudes and behaviors were not quite traditional but also not quite egalitarian. We have intentionally invoked that language here as the Transitional

Husbands class precisely fits the couples with transitional spouses that Hochschild and Machung describe in their ethnography.

Who are the people in the couples in each of the five housework classes? Chapter 5 first describes the couples based upon measures of the standard theoretical predictors of housework (for example, work hours for time availability) and then presents demographic portraits and comparisons of the classes. As expected, not only are the couples distinct in their housework profiles, but their demographic profiles also reflect how measures of power would be expected to be distributed should housework reflect power dynamics.

# 5

# Housework class characteristics

## Introduction

Chapter 4 presented the five classes: Ultra-Traditional, Traditional, Transitional Husbands, Egalitarian, and Egalitarian High Workload. To summarize briefly, Ultra-Traditional couples are characterized by a highly gendered division of labor, with wives spending substantial time on traditionally feminine tasks (but also the most time on masculine tasks as well). Traditional couples similarly perform housework using a gendered division of tasks but do not perform as much housework overall as do the Ultra-Traditional couples; as noted in Chapter 4, they are the largest class in our sample. Couples in the Transitional Husbands class reflect housework participation for both wives and husbands as generally in the middle of the distributions on tasks for the entire sample. Egalitarian couples have an almost equal split of housework time, with the gaps for both feminine and masculine tasks substantially smaller than in other classes. Finally, the Egalitarian High Workload couples are comprised of couples where husbands perform more housework than do wives and where both spouses spend approximately the same amount of time on feminine tasks.

In this chapter, we describe the classes by the key characteristics of the couples who comprise them. We begin by focusing on characteristics that are typically considered measures of the theoretical frameworks explaining the division of labor that were described in Chapters 1 and 2. We then compare the five classes based upon both couple and spousal demographic characteristics. After presenting the best fitting statistical model predicting class membership, the chapter concludes with our overall summaries of the five classes.

## Time availability

As noted in Chapters 1 and 2, this theoretical framework focuses on a simple economic perspective: individuals with less time available will do less housework and individuals with more time available will do more housework. Thus, the more time spent in the labor market, the less time an individual has to perform household labor.

As we can see from Table 5.1, there are substantial and statistically significant differences in work hours for both women and men across the five classes. Both women and men work the most hours in the Transitional Husbands class (and the total paid work hours for women and men combined is highest in this class). Statistically, however, the men in the Ultra-Traditional, Traditional, and Transitional Husbands classes have indistinguishable working hours. Among women, those in the Ultra-Traditional class work the fewest hours, which is a statistically significant difference from all other classes. Men in the Egalitarian High Workload class work the fewest hours among men and are statistically distinct from men in the Ultra-Traditional, Traditional, and Transitional Husbands classes. Women and men in the Ultra-Traditional class work the fewest combined hours.

**Table 5.1:** Class membership and average labor-market hours per week

|  | Ultra-Traditional | Traditional | Transitional Husbands | Egalitarian | Egalitarian High Workload |
|---|---|---|---|---|---|
| Woman's average weekly work hours | 10.6 | 21.6 | 29.8 | 25.0 | 26.5 |
| Man's average weekly work hours | 36.1 | 37.5 | 38.0 | 32.3 | 28.0 |

## Bargaining theory

Bargaining theory began as an approach that examines the influence of the resources of partners as reflections of power that they may be able to wield in the relationship. It became known as relative resources theory in the literature as much of the measurement focuses on the extent to which one partner's level of resources, relative to the other, enables them to get out of doing housework via the power attached to those resources. The mechanism at work in that interaction is that of bargaining: an individual with more resources is able to bargain their way out of housework due to the power accrued to the resource. Whether measured as absolute levels or relative levels, material resources are theorized to play an important role in determining the division of household work.

Comparing the five classes in terms of resources in Table 5.2, we find that women in the Ultra-Traditional class are statistically significantly distinct in that they have the fewest resources: they have the lowest income, educational attainment, and occupational prestige when employed (earnings and income values are expressed in 1987

**Table 5.2:** Class membership and absolute resources

| | Ultra-Traditional | Traditional | Transitional Husbands | Egalitarian | Egalitarian High Workload |
|---|---|---|---|---|---|
| Woman's earnings ($) | 3,304 | 10,055 | 14,276 | 9,684 | 9,721 |
| Man's earnings ($) | 24,874 | 27,852 | 23,889 | 20,205 | 14,634 |
| Woman's occupational prestige | 2,483 | 3,152 | 3,845 | 3,345 | 3,301 |
| Man's occupational prestige | 3,188 | 3,729 | 4,087 | 3,654 | 2,880 |
| Woman's educational attainment | 12.2 | 12.9 | 13.6 | 13.1 | 13.0 |
| Man's educational attainment | 12.2 | 13.1 | 13.8 | 13.0 | 12.7 |
| Woman's age | 40.9 | 39.7 | 34.2 | 38.4 | 36.8 |
| Man's age | 43.7 | 42.1 | 36.6 | 41.3 | 39.3 |
| Household income ($) | 31,664 | 41,968 | 40,895 | 33,564 | 28,548 |

dollars). This is consistent with bargaining theory's predictions that women with lower levels of resources will perform more household labor. Their husbands are also statistically distinct as they have the least formal education (and the second-lowest occupational prestige) of the five classes. Further, Ultra-Traditional men and women tend to be somewhat older than those in the other classes, which is a difference that is statistically significant. On the other hand, both women and men in the Transitional Husbands class have the highest earnings levels, highest educational attainment and occupational prestige (when employed), and tend to be younger. Somewhat consistent with bargaining theory's predictions is the low average occupational prestige among men in the Egalitarian High Workload class.

As women have historically had access to fewer material resources, relative resources have typically been measured by determining the woman's amount of the resource relative to her partner. In Table 5.3, we present that ratio for household income, occupational prestige, educational attainment, and age. For household income, the woman's relative income is calculated as the percentage of the total household income earned. For occupational prestige, we calculated two measures. The woman's relative occupational prestige is calculated for couples where the man is employed. Values greater than 1 are interpreted as the woman's occupational prestige being higher than that of the man's; values lower than 1 reflect the percentage of the man's value that the woman holds. The man's relative occupational prestige is calculated

**Table 5.3:** Class membership and relative resources

| | Ultra-Traditional | Traditional | Transitional Husbands | Egalitarian | Egalitarian High Workload |
|---|---|---|---|---|---|
| Woman's relative education | 1.047 | 1.027 | 1.024 | 1.051 | 1.073 |
| Woman's relative age | 0.941 | 0.946 | 0.940 | 0.938 | 0.946 |
| Woman's relative income | 0.114 | 0.244 | 0.341 | 0.304 | 0.345 |
| Woman's relative occupational prestige | 0.787 | 0.926 | 1.083 | 1.000 | 1.091 |
| Man's relative occupational prestige | 1.040 | 1.051 | 1.068 | 0.984 | 0.903 |

for couples where the woman is employed. In this case, values greater than 1 are interpreted as the man's occupational prestige being higher than that of the woman's; values lower than 1 reflect the percentage of the woman's value that the man holds. Both relative education and relative age are calculated as a ratio comparing the woman's value to the man's and are interpreted in the same way as the woman's relative occupational prestige is interpreted.

There are neither substantial nor statistical differences by class membership in women's relative education and age. Women statistically contribute the least to the couple's total income in the Ultra-Traditional class and the most in the Egalitarian High Workload and Transitional Husbands classes, distinguishing them from the Ultra-Traditional class. When men are employed, women hold significantly less prestigious jobs than do men in the Ultra-Traditional and Traditional class couples and more prestigious jobs in the Transitional Husbands and Egalitarian High Workload classes; women's and men's jobs have approximately the same prestige in the Egalitarian class. When women are employed, men hold significantly more prestigious jobs in Ultra-Traditional, Traditional, and Transitional Husbands couples. Again, men and women in the Egalitarian class hold jobs of approximately the same prestige and women have slightly more prestigious jobs in the Egalitarian High Workload class. When women in the Transitional Husbands class are employed, men's jobs are slightly more prestigious.

## Gender ideology

As noted in Chapter 2, a key social-psychological perspective explaining the division of household labor is called gender ideology (or separate spheres ideology). This framework argues that individuals who believe that there should be separate spheres for women, that men should do paid work and women only if necessary (if at all), and that women should be responsible for the private sphere (including housework and childcare) are more likely to behave accordingly.

Not surprisingly, Table 5.4 shows that both women and men in the Ultra-Traditional class are statistically distinct as they have the highest (most traditional) scores on our measure of gender ideology; in fact, more than a quarter (26.2 percent) of the Ultra-Traditional class couples have both partners scoring on the "traditional" category on our scale. This significant difference contrasts with the Transitional Husbands and the Egalitarian High Workload classes, where over one quarter of each class has both members on the "egalitarian" end of our scale.

There are two other patterns to note. First, couples' ideologies do not map cleanly with their behaviors. That is, there are couples who have at least one partner who falls into the "traditional" gender ideology category and who are part of either the Egalitarian or Egalitarian High Workload class. Similarly, there are couples who have at least one partner who falls into the "egalitarian" gender ideology category who

Table 5.4: Class membership and gender ideology

| | Ultra-Traditional | Traditional | Transitional Husbands | Egalitarian | Egalitarian High Workload |
|---|---|---|---|---|---|
| Woman's ideology score | 104.0 | 98.8 | 93.1 | 96.3 | 96.6 |
| Man's ideology score | 105.0 | 99.4 | 93.5 | 96.6 | 94.2 |
| **Couple ideology distribution** | | | | | |
| Both traditional | 26.2 | 16.2 | 8.9 | 10.8 | 12.0 |
| Both transitional | 16.8 | 18.7 | 12.6 | 19.3 | 15.1 |
| Both egalitarian | 5.1 | 15.9 | 27.1 | 18.6 | 27.7 |
| Woman traditional/ man transitional | 12.4 | 11.0 | 8.2 | 8.2 | 9.0 |
| Woman traditional/ man egalitarian | 3.6 | 3.6 | 2.9 | 4.9 | 3.0 |
| Woman transitional/ man traditional | 15.7 | 10.4 | 6.8 | 9.5 | 6.6 |
| Woman transitional/ man egalitarian | 7.5 | 10.9 | 15.2 | 13.1 | 15.7 |
| Woman egalitarian/ man traditional | 3.3 | 3.4 | 3.6 | 4.1 | 0 |
| Woman egalitarian/ man transitional | 8.1 | 9.9 | 14.7 | 11.3 | 10.8 |

are part of the Ultra-Traditional or Traditional class. The inconsistency between beliefs and behaviors is not unknown to scholars; indeed, much of Hochschild and Machung's (1989) previously mentioned book, entitled *The second shift* (a key scholarly publication for public consumption around the time that these data were collected), was dedicated to trying to make sense of the inconsistency in beliefs about gender and the actual work performed around the house.

Second, when women and men hold different gender ideologies, the couple belongs to a class that is somewhat more consistent with the man's gender ideology category than the woman's. In couples where women are "traditional" and men are "egalitarian," 7.2 percent of couples are either Ultra-Traditional or Traditional, whereas 7.9 percent are Egalitarian or Egalitarian High Workload. Alternatively, when men are "traditional" and women are "egalitarian," 6.7 percent of couples are Ultra-Traditional or Traditional and only 4.1 percent are Egalitarian, with no couples in the Egalitarian High Workload class. The same pattern is found when comparing when one spouse has a "transitional" and the other an "egalitarian" ideology (28.8 percent are Egalitarian or Egalitarian High Workload when the woman is "transitional" and the man is "egalitarian" but only 22.1 percent when the woman is "egalitarian" and the man is "transitional"). Approximately the same percentage of couples where one spouse has a "traditional" ideology and the other a "transitional" ideology are in the Ultra-Traditional or Traditional classes when summed together.

## Demographic characteristics of the classes

In this section, we examine who is in the classes based upon three types of characteristics: couple-level characteristics (Table 5.5); where the couple lives (Table 5.6); and individual partner characteristics (Table 5.7).

Couples in the Egalitarian High Workload class are most likely to be cohabiting (15.6 percent), while those in the Ultra-Traditional

**Table 5.5:** Class membership and couple characteristics

|  | Ultra-Traditional | Traditional | Transitional Husbands | Egalitarian | Egalitarian High Workload |
|---|---|---|---|---|---|
| Cohabiting | 5.1 | 8.2 | 11.8 | 11.1 | 15.6 |
| First marriage | 70.5 | 70.8 | 63.6 | 63.0 | 62.4 |
| Marital duration | 20.8 | 19.3 | 13.1 | 18.7 | 17.3 |
| Number of children | 1.458 | 0.926 | 0.99 | 0.988 | 1.251 |

**Table 5.6:** Class membership and geographic location

| | Ultra-Traditional | Traditional | Transitional Husbands | Egalitarian | Egalitarian High Workload |
|---|---|---|---|---|---|
| **Region of the country** | | | | | |
| Northeast | 16.1 | 18.9 | 18.1 | 20.0 | 16.7 |
| North Central | 32.1 | 30.0 | 29.2 | 24.9 | 29.6 |
| South | 32.7 | 34.3 | 30.6 | 32.5 | 35.1 |
| West | 19.1 | 16.8 | 21.9 | 22.6 | 18.4 |
| Live in metropolitan area | 63.7 | 74.4 | 81.2 | 75.1 | 78.8 |

**Table 5.7:** Class membership and partner demographic characteristics

| | Ultra-Traditional | Traditional | Transitional Husbands | Egalitarian | Egalitarian High Workload |
|---|---|---|---|---|---|
| **Woman's characteristics** | | | | | |
| *Race* | | | | | |
| White | 83.6 | 86.6 | 86.1 | 81.8 | 74.4 |
| Black | 8.1 | 7.3 | 7.7 | 10.6 | 19.3 |
| Hispanic | 7.2 | 4.6 | 3.9 | 6.1 | 4.5 |
| Other race | 1.0 | 1.4 | 2.3 | 1.4 | 1.7 |
| *Religion* | | | | | |
| Protestant | 67.1 | 65.2 | 57.7 | 60.1 | 65.1 |
| Catholic | 24.4 | 22.5 | 27.0 | 23.8 | 22.2 |
| Other religion | 2.5 | 4.5 | 4.1 | 5.0 | 4.5 |
| No religion | 5.8 | 7.5 | 11.0 | 10.9 | 8.0 |
| **Man's characteristics** | | | | | |
| *Race* | | | | | |
| White | 83.2 | 86.5 | 83.4 | 80.6 | 72.1 |
| Black | 8.2 | 7.5 | 8.9 | 12.1 | 19.5 |
| Hispanic | 7.1 | 4.7 | 5.2 | 5.7 | 6.7 |
| Other race | 1.3 | 1.2 | 2.5 | 1.6 | 1.7 |
| *Religion* | | | | | |
| Protestant | 61.8 | 60.7 | 54.5 | 60.2 | 57.5 |
| Catholic | 23.6 | 23.1 | 25.9 | 22.2 | 24.5 |
| Other religion | 1.6 | 2.1 | 1.8 | 2.6 | 2.2 |
| No religion | 11.2 | 11.0 | 15.4 | 11.9 | 15.0 |

class are least likely (5.1 percent), which is a statistically significant difference. Ultra-Traditional class couples have been married longer and have significantly more children than the other four classes; Ultra-Traditional class and Traditional class couples are significantly more likely to be in first marriages than the others.

There are no substantial differences in geographic location between classes, but couples in the Ultra-Traditional class are statistically less likely to live in a metropolitan area than are other couples.

Egalitarian and Egalitarian High Workload class couples are somewhat more likely to be non-white than are the other classes; this difference is statistically significant. Consistent with other research from the 1980s (Roof and Hoge, 1980), men are less likely to profess a religious preference than are women; this is slightly more likely in Transitional Husbands and Egalitarian High Workload class couples. There are few differences in the classes based on women's religious preference, though couples in the Transitional Husbands class have a somewhat higher percentage of women who are Catholic (27 percent) than do other classes, which is a difference that is statistically significant.

## Predicting housework class membership

The previous analyses have examined differences in class membership one characteristic at a time. Table 5.8 presents the results of the best fitting statistical model that includes multiple characteristics, or predictors, simultaneously. To do this, we employ multinomial logistic regression using Traditional class membership as the reference category. Rather than present statistical coefficients, we present the odds ratios resulting from our analysis. Here, odds ratios are interpreted as the odds that a couple will be classified as the specific class (for example, Ultra-Traditional) versus being classified as Traditional given a change in a particular predictor (for example, an increase in the wife's working hours), net the effects of all of the other characteristics included in the model. That is, if the odds ratio is greater than 1, then an increase in the predictor increases the likelihood of being in the specific class relative to the Traditional class; if the odds ratio is less than 1, then an increase in the predictor decreases the likelihood of being in the specific class relative to the Traditional class.

The best fitting statistical model includes measures of time availability, absolute and relative resources, and gender ideology, as well as couple- and individual-level demographic characteristics. The measures included are all statistically significant predictors of differentiating across the housework classes. We have chosen to

**Table 5.8:** Predicting class membership

| Characteristic | Ultra-Traditional (versus Traditional) | Transitional Husbands (versus Traditional) | Egalitarian (versus Traditional) | Egalitarian High Workload (versus Traditional) |
|---|---|---|---|---|
| *Time availability* | | | | |
| Woman's average weekly work hours | 0.978* | 1.012* | 1.007 | 1.009 |
| Man's average weekly work hours | 1.006 | 0.990* | 0.981* | 0.979* |
| *Absolute resources* | | | | |
| Woman's occupational prestige | 0.999* | 1.001* | 1.000 | 0.999 |
| Man's occupational prestige | 0.999* | 1.001* | 1.000 | 0.999 |
| Woman's age | 0.995 | 0.966* | 0.986* | 0.983 |
| *Relative resources* | | | | |
| Woman's relative income | 0.292* | 1.355 | 1.256 | 0.921 |
| *Gender ideology* | | | | |
| Man's ideology score | 1.014* | 0.985* | 0.988* | 0.979* |
| *Couple characteristics* | | | | |
| Cohabiting | 0.850 | 0.877 | 0.963 | 2.418* |
| Number of children | 1.428* | 1.064 | 1.082 | 1.328* |
| *Demographic characteristics* | | | | |
| Man's race (reference = white) | | | | |
| Black | 1.340 | 1.251 | 1.533* | 3.884* |
| Hispanic | 0.823 | 1.092 | 1.597 | 1.455 |
| Other race | 1.497 | 4.767* | 5.183* | 5.335* |

Note: *$p$ < .05.

present the odds relative to the Traditional class as they are the largest class in the sample. The model presented here includes theoretical predictors as well as demographic characteristics, and confirms the descriptive analysis presented earlier in the chapter. Compared to couples classified as Traditional, those couples classified as Ultra-Traditional are characterized by women who work fewer hours, lower occupational prestige among both partners, women with lower relative incomes, men who hold more "traditional" gender ideologies, and more children. Compared to couples classified as Traditional, those classified as part of the Transitional Husbands class are characterized by women who work more hours, men who work fewer hours, higher occupational prestige among both partners, younger women, men who hold more "egalitarian" gender ideologies, and men of "another race" (other than white, black, and Hispanic). Compared to couples classified as Traditional, those classified as Egalitarian are characterized by men who work fewer hours, younger women, men who hold more "egalitarian" gender ideologies, and men who are black or "another race". Finally, compared to couples classified as Traditional, couples classified as Egalitarian High Workload are characterized by men who work fewer hours, men who hold more "egalitarian" gender ideologies, cohabiters, and men who are black or "another race."

## Summary

In this chapter, we have examined similarities and differences across the five classes based upon not only demographic characteristics, but also measures of the key theoretical predictors of housework performance, both as individual characteristics and then simultaneously through statistical analysis. First, we summarize the most distinctive differences between the classes. Women in the Ultra-Traditional class tend to work far fewer hours outside the home than those of the other four classes and consequently tend to have much lower earnings and lower occupational prestige. Men in the Egalitarian High Workload class tend to work the fewest hours and have the lowest earnings and occupational prestige of the five classes. Women in the Transitional Husbands class work the most hours and have the highest earnings, occupational prestige, and educational attainment. Women in the Transitional Husbands and Egalitarian High Workload classes have the highest relative incomes. Women and men hold jobs of approximately the same prestige in the Egalitarian class but in no other class. Both women and men in the Ultra-Traditional class have the most traditional ideologies, while both women and men in the Transitional Husbands class have the least traditional (most egalitarian) ideologies. That couples who do not have the same gender ideology are more likely to belong to a class that is consistent with the man's ideology is an example of latent or hidden power. The fact that couples in which one spouse holds a "traditional" gender ideology and the other holds as "transitional" ideology are similar in their distribution across classes (but more likely to be toward the traditional split of the division of labor) provides evidence of the historic connections between traditional gender ideologies and traditional divisions of labor; falling into a traditional division of labor is the path of least resistance for these couples. Couples in the Egalitarian High Workload class are the most likely to be cohabiting, while couples in the Ultra-Traditional class are the least likely to do so. Spouses in the Egalitarian High Workload class are far more likely to be persons of color than in the other groups.

Our analysis has documented the importance of all of the theoretical frameworks as mechanisms through which to understand the distribution of housework within and across couples. Our overarching argument is that the performance of housework can be seen as a proxy for power dynamics within couples. The analysis in this chapter has demonstrated that the typical resources that reflect power in the public sphere (for example, income, occupational prestige, and educational attainment) are utilized by individuals within the social exchange of relationships to opt out of performing certain work in their home. These resources are gendered in that men's resources tend to be able to allow them to get more out of the social exchange, that is, to do less housework per type of resource exchanged in the relationship. The power attributed to resources important in a capitalist economy is gendered power as men's association with the public sphere when these data were collected was only just coming under cultural scrutiny. Thus, the patterns of the distribution of economic and social resources across the five classes are consistent with how we would expect all types of power to operate. Men's ability to draw on those economic and social resources reflects their exertion of latent and hidden power in their relationships, whereby the social institutional arrangements that support men's greater economic opportunities in the public sphere spill over into the private sphere, making it seem natural and normal for them to perform less housework overall, and fewer feminine tasks in particular. That the connection between those economic and social resources and men's housework performance is typically stronger in households with a more traditionally gendered division of housework (for example, the Ultra-Traditional and Traditional couples) is further evidence of men's ability to leverage latent and hidden power at home.

The Egalitarian High Workload class reflects not only a significant contribution of time from the spouses on housework, but also husbands who spend the least amount of time in paid work (28 hours per week compared to 36 hours for the entire sample of couples). Not surprisingly, wives in these couples earned the greatest percentage of income of the five groups (35 percent compared to a sample average of 24 percent). We consider this class a vanguard group as their paid and unpaid labor, their resource distribution, and their overall general behaviors (for example, being more likely to cohabit) are suggestive of what couples in the U.S. could look like if both men and women are given the opportunity to pay equal attention to both paid and unpaid labor, as well as their work and family lives. The question becomes whether this class increases, decreases, or stays the same over time, especially over the time period between Waves 1 and 2 of the National

Survey of Families and Households (NSFH). In Chapter 7, we present findings from a longitudinal analysis, called latent trajectory analysis, which examines precisely this question. However, before we talk about stability or change over time in the classes, Chapter 6 highlights a series of tests of our argument regarding the use of housework as a proxy for power dynamics in couples by comparing the extent to which spouses have been able to shape one another's labor-market participation and the presence of conflict and physical violence across the classes.

# 6

# Housework class consequences

## Introduction

The key goal of this book is to demonstrate that understanding the division of housework in couples can provide insights into the power dynamics of the couple. In Chapter 5, we documented how individual characteristics and resources that are afforded power in the public sphere are distributed within and across the five housework classes. In the classes characterized by a more traditionally gendered division of housework time and task division, men are more likely to exhibit characteristics or hold more resources that reflect power in the public sphere, such as income and education. In these classes, men perform less housework than do women and perform traditionally masculine tasks when they do perform housework. Further, in the couples in classes where housework is connected less rigidly to gender, women exhibit more characteristics or hold more resources that reflect power in the public sphere. The division of labor captured by the categorization into the five classes demonstrates how men and women are exerting latent and/or hidden power (that is, how one partner is able to indirectly influence the other partner's behavior, including the ability to keep issues from rising to the level of conflict) through the mobilization of resources. This is not an exacting set of associations, as we noted in Chapter 5. However, these patterns provide support for our claim that housework and power dynamics are intimately intertwined.

Power dynamics have substantial implications within couples and can be exhibited through latent and hidden power, or through overt power (as in the physical or psychological manipulation of the other partner). In this chapter, we compare two arenas where power is exerted in couples: the economic sphere of influence (with latent and hidden power as the mechanisms); and conflict (measured as disagreements and physical violence). Comparing the distribution of perceptions and reported behaviors across the classes provides convincing evidence that housework can be considered a proxy for power.

## Preferred labor-market hours

Latent and hidden power can be evidenced in other forms of family dynamics beyond housework. Paid employment hours reflect financial need within a household but can also be considered one means of demonstrating masculinity and femininity based on contemporary U.S. gender norms. The literature on under- and over-employment has documented patterns in how individuals work more or fewer hours in the labor market than their education and other skills would imply due to other characteristics, including gender and marital status (for example, Reynolds, 2003). Reporting working more or fewer hours than one would like could reflect a mismatch between the individual's skills and the local labor market's job opportunities. It could also reflect a power dynamic inside the household where one partner actively discourages another from working additional hours in the paid labor market and is able to exert latent power in the form of suppressing labor-market participation. We would expect this to be more likely to occur in couples where there is the expectation of equality in the relationship: that women would exert latent power to discourage men from working more within the paid labor market in order for there to be greater parity within the household, or that men would encourage women to work more for the same reason. If this theoretical argument holds, we would expect to find that men are working fewer hours than they want and women are working more hours than they want among couples in the Transitional Husbands, Egalitarian, and Egalitarian High Workload classes. Wives would report that they would want their husbands to be working fewer hours and husbands would report they would want their wives to be working more hours in these households *if* latent power is *not* being exerted. That is, if power is being exerted, the work hours are more like what the partner wants than what the respondent wants, and if power is not being exerted among the couples in the Transitional Husbands, Egalitarian, and Egalitarian High Workload classes, there is a greater likelihood to report wanting to see different hours of employment among one's spouse.

However, wanting to work more or fewer hours may also reflect the complex negotiations of power within the household that are in response to external forces. For example, it is possible that among couples where there is an expected gendered division of paid and unpaid work along more traditional lines, both women and men may want men to work more and women to work less but there are no jobs that would facilitate this arrangement. We would then be unlikely to see that men are able to exert latent power over their spouse's labor-market hours where wives work approximately the same hours as their husbands want them to but not more. In fact, in the face of structural constraints where employment for traditional men is scarce, research has shown that men engage in gender-deviance neutralization (Greenstein, 2000), where they refuse to perform tasks (including both paid work and housework) that they perceive may undermine their masculinity (Rubin, 1976). Thus, we recognize that our analysis of the concordance of preferred and actual labor-market hours across the housework classes may not capture the full picture of how latent power is exerted within couples, or the extent to which partners acquiesce to power being exerted.

One analysis of the complex negotiation between preferred and actual labor-market hours for oneself and one's spouse is presented in Table 6.1. Both spouses were asked about their own actual and preferred labor-market hours, as well as the hours they preferred for their spouse. The difference between preferred and actual hours is constructed by subtracting actual hours from preferred hours. Positive values mean that the person prefers more hours to be worked, and negative values mean that the person prefers fewer hours to be worked than are actually being worked.

There is some evidence of spouses using latent and hidden power to shape one another's labor-market experience and of spouses acquiescing to this exercise of power. Ultra-Traditional women report preferring to work more than they do while their husbands want them to work even fewer hours than they currently work, with both being statistically significant differences. The struggle around women's participation in the public sphere through labor-market hours in these couples is consistent with the cultural uniqueness of this group in the private sphere. Ultra-Traditional husbands seem to want an almost completely gendered split of responsibilities for paid and unpaid work: for them to be sole breadwinners and their wives to focus only on the home. Their connection to the prevailing cultural norms around breadwinning would allow them to exert this latent and/or hidden power in ways that seem natural in their interactions.

Traditional couples' preferences are consistent with what we would expect for couples attempting to model a contemporary division of paid and unpaid work that continues to reflect some gender differentiation in the public and private spheres. Both spouses would prefer men to work more, and while Traditional women are comfortable with their labor-market hours, Traditional men would prefer a small increase in their wives' paid work time.

**Table 6.1:** Class membership and preferred labor-market hours

| | Ultra-Traditional | Traditional | Transitional Husbands | Egalitarian | Egalitarian High Workload |
|---|---|---|---|---|---|
| Woman's average weekly work hours | 10.6 | 21.6 | 29.8 | 25.0 | 26.5 |
| Man's average weekly work hours | 36.1 | 37.5 | 38.0 | 32.3 | 28.0 |
| Woman's preferred working hours | 18.6 | 21.1 | 23.2 | 22.9 | 25.1 |
| Difference between woman's preferred and actual working hours | 7.9 | 0.5 | 6.5 | 2.2 | 1.6 |
| Woman's preferred working hours for man | 32.5 | 32.2 | 33.4 | 30.5 | 31.6 |
| Difference between preferred and actual working hours for man as reported by woman | 3.8 | 5.6 | 4.7 | 2.5 | −3.4 |
| Man's preferred working hours | 33.6 | 33.7 | 34.5 | 33.5 | 34.3 |
| Difference between man's preferred and actual working hours | 2.6 | 3.9 | 3.9 | −1.3 | −6.1 |
| Man's preferred working hours for woman | 16.0 | 19.1 | 21.1 | 20.6 | 21.5 |
| Difference between preferred and actual working hours for woman as reported by man | −5.2 | 2.6 | 8.7 | 4.1 | 4.9 |

Couples in the Transitional Husbands and Egalitarian High Workload classes are internally consistent with one another, as well as with what we would expect of their labor-market preferences conceptually. Within the Transitional Husbands class, both spouses want women to have more paid work time and for men to have a slight increase in paid work hours. As these couples have negotiated a division of labor where men are performing somewhat more housework than do Traditional men, it stands to reason that they would expect women to change their contributions to the social exchange by increasing their labor-market hours. Similarly, couples in the Egalitarian High Workload class report a desired small increase in women's labor-market hours and a reduction in men's labor-market hours, perhaps to accommodate men's high levels of unpaid labor. Rather than reflect the use of latent or hidden power, couples in the Transitional Husbands and Egalitarian High Workload classes seem to be working toward creating consistency in their behavior in the work and non-work spheres. There is some evidence for this shift toward behavioral consistency among couples in the Egalitarian class as well (that is, men's desire to work less and for their wives to work more). Overall, however, there is little evidence of latent power over labor-market experiences among couples in the Transitional Husbands, Egalitarian, and Egalitarian High Workload classes.

The results in Table 6.1 focus on whether there are differences in preferred labor-market hours across the five classes, without taking into consideration any other factors that may influence either class membership or preferred labor-market hours—or both. Table 6.2 reports the results of a series of path analysis models, structured largely as depicted in Figure 6.1. We regress each measure of preferred labor-market hours on individual-level and couple-level predictors *and* class membership simultaneously while also taking into consideration how individual- and couple-level predictors shape class membership (for more details on these statistical models, see the Appendix).

Table 6.2 describes the results of the best fitting statistical models for each of the eight preferred labor-market hours outcomes. We note whether the outcome differs significantly by class membership net of other characteristics included in the model. As before, the Traditional class is the reference category. As noted in the Appendix, we do not present coefficients, but rather whether the differences in preferred labor-market hours reported in Table 6.1 reflect significant differences between couples in the Traditional class and the other classes overall (for a list of all other characteristics included in each best fitting model, see Table A3 in the Appendix).

**Figure 6.1:** Multivariate modeling strategy for housework class consequences

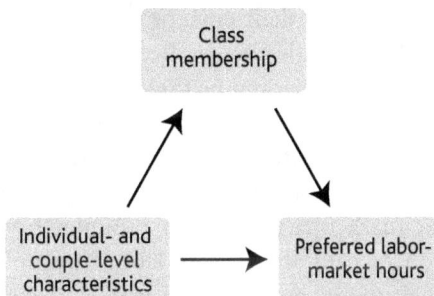

**Table 6.2:** Results of multivariate models predicting preferred labor-market hours outcomes

| Outcome | Effect of class membership statistically significant? |
|---|---|
| Woman's preferred working hours | Yes |
| Difference between woman's preferred and actual working hours | Yes |
| Woman's preferred working hours for man | No |
| Difference between preferred and actual working hours for man as reported by woman | Yes |
| Man's preferred working hours | No |
| Difference between man's preferred and actual working hours | No |
| Man's preferred working hours for woman | Yes |
| Difference between preferred and actual working hours for woman as reported by man | Yes |

The multivariate analyses confirm the results shown in Table 6.1. There are significant differences across the classes in five of the preferred labor-market hours outcomes net of the influence of individual-level and couple-level characteristics. Four of the five class differences are centered around women's labor-market participation (each spouse's preference for women in the labor market and the difference between the preference and actual labor-market hours). There may be an attempt by Ultra-Traditional men to wield latent power in order to have their homes reflect the ideal-type of a "traditional" American home from the 1950s, à la "Leave it to Beaver," as is evidenced by the overall significant differences across classes in Ultra-Traditional women's preference for working more hours and their husbands' preference for them working less. This potential desire to connect to what was still a prevailing cultural norm when the data were collected would be seen as natural, as would the exertion of latent power to enact those beliefs. The overall difference in women's preferred working hours (and difference from their current working hours) for women in the Transitional Husbands class by both spouses is significant net of other characteristics, providing further evidence of the underlying expectations of these couples to balance men's increased participation at home with women's greater economic contributions in the labor market. The findings in Tables 6.1 and 6.2 highlight the central nature of women's labor-market participation in couples' navigation of their collective division of paid and unpaid labor, not unlike the culture overall during the time when these data were collected.

# Reports of disagreements

Disagreements occur in relationships. The frequency with which they occur could reflect the power dynamics in the relationship as disagreements could be indicative of a power struggle between partners. The National Survey of Families and Households (NSFH) measures disagreements by asking about how often in the past year respondents and their spouses disagreed over household tasks, money, spending time together, sex, the children, and in-laws. Having another child was also listed; however, given the age of our sample and the resulting minimal variability of responses, we chose not to include that item in our analysis. We first constructed an additive score of the overall number of disagreements, where higher values reflect more overall disagreements. We then evaluated class differences in the frequency of specific disagreements. Those values are reported in Table 6.3 as whether or not the woman or man says they disagreed about the item at least several times a month (for example, 22.6 percent of women in

**Table 6.3**: Class membership and reports of disagreements

| | Ultra-Traditional | Traditional | Transitional Husbands | Egalitarian | Egalitarian High Workload |
|---|---|---|---|---|---|
| Woman's overall disagreement score | 5.3 | 4.4 | 5.4 | 4.8 | 6.4 |
| *Woman's reports (%) of disagreement about:* | | | | | |
| Household tasks | 22.6 | 18.8 | 24.2 | 25.0 | 24.3 |
| Money | 24.6 | 18.9 | 29.0 | 25.5 | 33.3 |
| Spending time together | 19.4 | 18.9 | 26.9 | 19.2 | 33.7 |
| Sex | 15.7 | 13.6 | 19.9 | 18.0 | 28.4 |
| Children | 28.4 | 24.9 | 36.3 | 35.0 | 41.6 |
| In-laws | 11.4 | 7.5 | 10.9 | 8.3 | 16.0 |
| Man's overall disagreement score | 5.0 | 4.4 | 5.5 | 5.4 | 5.8 |
| *Man's reports (%) of disagreement about:* | | | | | |
| Household tasks | 20.9 | 19.4 | 26.5 | 26.2 | 19.1 |
| Money | 26.3 | 20.4 | 32.3 | 27.0 | 25.5 |
| Spending time together | 24.4 | 20.2 | 31.7 | 26.0 | 40.0 |
| Sex | 19.5 | 17.5 | 24.7 | 24.3 | 25.8 |
| Children | 24.7 | 23.9 | 33.1 | 28.9 | 21.8 |
| In-laws | 10.2 | 9.3 | 14.0 | 11.2 | 11.7 |

the Ultra-Traditional class report that they disagree about household tasks at least several times a month).

The Egalitarian High Workload class reports the most overall disagreements, making them statistically distinct from all other classes. Not surprisingly, given that this class is characterized by both spouses performing substantial amounts of housework, they also report the most frequent disagreements over spending time together. Consistent with other published scholarship (Wilcox and Nock, 2006), couples in the Traditional class report the lowest overall disagreements and the lowest frequency of specific disagreements in almost every category for both women and men. The Traditional class represents a cultural norm in how the private sphere is organized, yielding an easier roadmap for couples (Wilcox and Nock, 2006). The Ultra-Traditional class reports slightly more frequent disagreements than the Traditional class; this is perhaps due to men using verbal disagreements to maintain their strict gendered boundaries and expectations within the household. However, the reported differences in both Ultra-Traditional and Traditional women's and men's overall reports of disagreements are not statistically distinct from one another, emphasizing the power of the cultural norm of separate spheres and the roles that women and men play in the maintenance of the private sphere. On the whole, there are significant differences in women's reports of all disagreements across the five classes, and the five classes differ significantly in the frequency of men's reports of disagreements for all but disagreements over in-laws.

Table 6.4 describes whether class membership is a statistically significant predictor of women's and men's overall disagreement scores and frequency of reporting specific disagreements in multivariate models, as depicted in Figure 6.1. As before, we do not present coefficients, but rather whether the differences in reports of disagreements reported in Table 6.3 reflect statistically significant differences overall (for a list of all other characteristics included in each best fitting model, see Table A3 in the Appendix).

There were significant differences in reports of disagreements for both women and men based on class membership, net of other individual-level and couple-level characteristics. Broadly, the results in Table 6.4 reinforce the distinctive nature of the Egalitarian High Workload class as they are significantly more likely to report more disagreements (see Table 6.3). These multivariate findings provide evidence that the housework dynamics in this unusual class of couples are difficult to maintain, in part, due to the fact that the couples are challenging culturally normative behavioral expectations. The

**Table 6.4:** Results of multivariate models predicting reports of disagreements

| Outcome | Effect of class membership statistically significant? |
|---|---|
| Woman's overall disagreement score | Yes |
| *Woman's reports (%) of disagreement about:* | |
| Household tasks | Yes |
| Money | Yes |
| Spending time together | No |
| Sex | No |
| Children | Yes |
| In-laws | Yes |
| Man's overall disagreement score | Yes |
| *Man's reports (%) of disagreement about:* | |
| Household tasks | No |
| Money | Yes |
| Spending time together | Yes |
| Sex | No |
| Children | No |
| In-laws | No |

Egalitarian High Workload couples are not more likely to disagree over household tasks than are couples in other classes, though Traditional women are simply less likely to report disagreements over their household division of labor, likely due to cultural norms supporting the household arrangements. However, with a high level of mutual focus on the household as their defining characteristic, the distinctiveness of the couples means that they had fewer cultural roadmaps to follow and fewer structural supports, and were therefore likely to have disagreements. Most importantly, they were more likely to report disagreements, net of other characteristics, signaling the willingness of the spouses to actively engage in constant negotiation and reinforcement of how they organized their household. These findings support our argument that household labor configurations can be seen as a proxy for power dynamics. Household labor configurations, as noted in Chapter 2, are fraught with cultural expectations of gender and power. These findings demonstrate that when household labor configurations are far from the cultural norm, there will be an increase in the likelihood that couples will actively construct, and will be comfortable with actively constructing, their own local norms and power configurations.

Interestingly, the two areas where there were no differences among women's reports once other characteristics were taken into account (reporting disagreement in spending time together and sex) were the only two areas where there were class membership differences in men's reports of disagreements. Net of other characteristics, Egalitarian High Workload men were significantly more likely to report disagreements about spending time together than were men in other classes. As noted earlier, this is likely due to the active negotiations among the couples in this class around how to maintain their unusual configuration. What is notable is that while both spouses report more disagreements about spending time together, it is the men rather than the women who are statistically distinct from those in other classes. That men are significantly more likely to report disagreements about spending time together reflects their active participation in the unusual configuration of their household. What is unknown is whether these disagreements reflect men's (or women's) desires to spend more or less time together given the sheer volume of housework that these couples perform.

Table 6.3 notes that men in the Ultra-Traditional and Traditional classes are less likely than men in other classes to report disagreements about sex; the multivariate analysis confirms statistical differences across classes net of other individual-level and couple-level characteristics. There are two possible explanations for this set of findings. First, due to cultural norms and expectations around sexual relations, couples in the Ultra-Traditional and Traditional classes may simply have fewer disagreements about sex. Men are the sexual initiators and women comply. Couples in other classes may be more likely to have disagreements as both women and men negotiate women's sexual agency. The second possible explanation is that there are no differences in the actual frequency of disagreements about sex, but that Ultra-Traditional and Traditional couples are less likely to report differences because of their internalized understandings of sexual relations in couples: men are supposed to initiate sexual relations when they want and women are supposed to comply. Men in the Ultra-Traditional and Traditional classes would possibly be embarrassed if disagreements occurred as this would suggest that they are not living up to those expectations. As there are no statistical differences by class membership in women's reports of the frequency of disagreements over sex, this is a plausible explanation.

## Conflict resolution tactics

When couples disagree, they have a variety of conflict resolution tactics that they can use. These tactics may reflect power dynamics within the couple. Using items from the Conflict Tactics Scale (Straus, 1979), respondents were given the following prompt: "Here are various ways that couples deal with serious disagreements. When you have a serious disagreement with your partner, how often do you[:] keep your opinion to yourself, discuss disagreements calmly, argue heatedly or shout at each other, end up hitting or throwing things at each other." We report on how spouses say they typically address disagreement when it occurs. Table 6.5 documents whether a woman or man reports that they at least sometimes use a particular tactic to resolve conflict, for example, 13.6 percent of women in the Egalitarian High Workload class reported at least sometimes keeping their opinions to themselves.

There are very few differences across classes in either women's or men's reports of conflict resolution tactics. Women in Ultra-Traditional couples are significantly more likely to keep their opinions to themselves than are any other women. Men in Egalitarian couples are least likely to keep their opinions to themselves than are any other men; their reports are quite similar to the reports of women in those couples. This is evidence of equality of power in those couples in that

**Table 6.5:** Class membership and conflict resolution tactics

|  | Ultra-Traditional | Traditional | Transitional Husbands | Egalitarian | Egalitarian High Workload |
|---|---|---|---|---|---|
| *Woman reports (%) of:* |  |  |  |  |  |
| Keeping opinions to self | 22.3 | 16.2 | 15.9 | 16.5 | 13.6 |
| Discussing disagreements calmly | 44.6 | 40.8 | 41.2 | 43.6 | 48.5 |
| Argue heatedly or shout at each other | 6.4 | 7.8 | 9.2 | 7.7 | 8.6 |
| End up hitting or throwing things at each other | 0.4 | 0.4 | 0 | 0.4 | 0 |
| *Man reports (%) of:* |  |  |  |  |  |
| Keeping opinions to self | 23.7 | 22.1 | 21.2 | 18.1 | 24.2 |
| Discussing disagreements calmly | 47.3 | 47.3 | 43.6 | 46.7 | 51.1 |
| Argue heatedly or shout at each other | 5.8 | 4.9 | 6.6 | 6.1 | 7.4 |
| End up hitting or throwing things at each other | 0.6 | 0.2 | 0 | 0.8 | 0 |

both men and women are equally comfortable sharing their opinions during disagreements.

Table 6.6 reports whether class membership significantly predicts the six conflict resolution tactics for women and men net of individual- and couple-level characteristics. As in Table 6.4, Table 6.6 presents the results of the analyses performed for conflict resolution tactics using multivariate models, as depicted in Figure 6.1 (for a list of all other characteristics included in each best fitting model, see Table A3 in the Appendix).

The multivariate results reaffirm the descriptive findings in Table 6.5: there are few differences across classes in conflict resolution tactics. In fact, there are no class membership differences in men's reports of conflict resolution tactics. Despite the finding that men in Egalitarian couples are least likely to keep their opinions to themselves relative to other couples, this difference is not statistically significant once other factors are considered.

There are two differences based on class membership in women's reports once other characteristics are considered: keeping opinions to oneself and discussing disagreements calmly. As noted earlier, this suggests that the increased likelihood of women in the Ultra-Traditional couples keeping their opinions to themselves is indicative of the dynamics within the couples (rather than the selection of individuals based on characteristics into the classes). These women may be performing emphasized femininity (Connell, 1987), whereby they behave in a manner that reinforces stereotypical cultural norms about gender in the relationship. By silencing themselves in response to their husbands' behaviors, they are reaffirming the culturally traditional patterns of gendered behaviors and power dynamics. This behavior is

**Table 6.6:** Results of multivariate models predicting conflict resolution tactics

| Outcome | Class membership statistically significant? |
|---|---|
| *Woman reports (%) of:* | |
| Keeping opinions to self | Yes |
| Discussing disagreements calmly | Yes |
| Argue heatedly or shout at each other | No |
| End up hitting or throwing things at each other | No |
| *Man reports (%) of:* | |
| Keeping opinions to self | No |
| Discussing disagreements calmly | No |
| Argue heatedly or shout at each other | No |
| End up hitting or throwing things at each other | No |

consistent with our expectations if housework is seen as a proxy for power dynamics.

Interestingly, while women in the Egalitarian High Workload couples report the highest number of disagreements, the multivariate analyses show that they are also significantly more likely to report that they discuss disagreements calmly. Despite the finding that these couples have more disagreements—again, likely because of the minimal structural supports for their unusual household configuration—they are more likely to calmly discuss the situation that has led to the disagreement than are couples in other classes. This result provides additional evidence of the uniqueness of the couples in the Egalitarian High Workload class but again reflects the extent to which couples outside of the cultural norm are comfortable with actively constructing their own power configurations.

## Intimate partner violence

One conflict resolution tactic that has previously been connected to the expression of power is intimate partner violence (Atkinson et al, 2005). Intimate partner violence reflects the exertion of power in a relationship, especially when perpetrated by men (Hattery, 2008). While women have been documented to initiate intimate partner violence, research often shows that women's violent behavior can typically be considered self-defense or retaliation for violence or threats of violence by their partner (Bair-Merritt et al, 2010).

Ultra-Traditional and Traditional couples are expected to have more reports of intimate partner violence and more reports of violence where women were injured than are other classes of couples. These two classes reflect a gendered power dynamic where men have been able to avoid performing housework. We expect that these men are also more willing than other groups to use physical violence to exert power in their relationships, as has been found in previous scholarship (Atkinson et al, 2005). If arguments do become physical in Egalitarian and Egalitarian High Workload couples, we expect that there will be similar reports by women and men as to the originator/perpetrator of the violence.

We measured intimate partner violence in the five classes based upon responses to the question "Sometimes arguments between partners become physical. During the last year has this happened in arguments between you and your partner?" Among individuals who reported that an argument became physical, we report the number of fights during which the spouses hit, shoved, or threw things at one another. We also document whether either spouse was ever cut, bruised, or seriously injured in an argument. All of these reports are presented based upon both the woman's and the man's responses.

Consistent with previous scholarship, very few individuals report that an argument became physical in the year prior to the survey. In many ways, this is good in that, overall, few couples were experiencing intimate partner violence. Women in the Traditional class were significantly less likely than women in any other class to report that they had a physical argument in the past year. Women in the Egalitarian class were just as likely as women in the Transitional Husbands class to report a physical argument in the past year, and men in the Ultra-Traditional class were just as likely as men in the Transitional Husbands class.

The numbers in parentheses in Table 6.7 are the numbers of respondents who said that at least one argument had become physical; the reports of the number of arguments where a spouse was injured is based on reports from only those individuals who reported that an argument had become physical. As there were so few reports in the Egalitarian High Workload class, we caution strict comparisons between them and other classes. Men in the Ultra-Traditional class report fewer physical arguments than do women in the Ultra-Traditional class. However, men overall reported more fights where women hit, shoved, or threw things at men than did women across all classes and fewer fights where men hit, shoved, or threw things at women than did women. Therefore, looking solely at men's reports, it would seem that women were significantly more violent than were men in relationships in the Traditional, Transitional Husbands, and Egalitarian classes. Examining only women's reports suggests that men across all classes were slightly more likely to be violent than were women, with the reports becoming more disparate from one another the more traditional the division of labor was distributed between the spouses.

Finally, we examined reports of whether the woman or man were ever injured in an argument based on each spouse's reports. As might be expected, in all classes (except the Egalitarian High Workload class), women reported being injured more frequently than they reported men being injured. Men in the Ultra-Traditional and Traditional classes reported that women and men were injured at the same rate, whereas men in the Egalitarian class were substantially more likely to report being injured than were their wives. There are similarities within class on reports of men being injured in the Ultra-Traditional, Traditional, and Transitional Husbands classes. However, within

**Table 6.7:** Class membership and physical violence

| | Ultra-Traditional | Traditional | Transitional Husbands | Egalitarian | Egalitarian High Workload |
|---|---|---|---|---|---|
| *Woman reports of:* | | | | | |
| Physical argument in the last year (%) | 4.0 | 2.8 | 5.9 | 6.0 | 4.9 |
| Number of fights woman hit, shoved, or threw things at man | 0.74 (23) | 0.84 (44) | 0.57 (21) | 0.94 (13) | 0.17 (6) |
| Was man ever cut, bruised, or seriously injured in an argument? | 8.3 | 13.3 | 9.5 | 17.6 | 16.7 |
| Number of fights man hit, shoved, or threw things at woman | 1.17 (23) | 1.23 (44) | 0.86 (21) | 1.12 (13) | 0.33 (6) |
| Was woman ever cut, bruised, or seriously injured in an argument? | 38.0 | 22.2 | 19.0 | 23.5 | 0 |
| *Man reports of:* | | | | | |
| Physical argument in the last year (%) | 4.6 | 3.5 | 4.9 | 3.5 | 4.2 |
| Number of fights woman hit, shoved, or threw things at man | 0 (27) | 1.17 (54) | 1.19 (16) | 1.23 (13) | 1.00 (4) |
| Was man ever cut, bruised, or seriously injured in an argument? | 14.8 | 11.1 | 6.2 | 30.8 | 0 |
| Number of fights man hit, shoved, or threw things at woman | 0.15 (27) | 0.70 (54) | 0.63 (16) | 0.77 (13) | 1.00 (4) |
| Was woman ever cut, bruised, or seriously injured in an argument? | 14.8 | 11.1 | 0 | 15.4 | 25.0 |

each class, women and men differed widely on whether women were injured in an argument, with women generally reporting more instances of injury than men.

Table 6.8 documents whether class membership significantly predicts the six conflict resolution tactics for women and men net of individual- and couple-level characteristics. As in Table 6.6, Table 6.8 presents

**Table 6.8:** Results of multivariate models predicting intimate partner violence

| Outcome | Class membership statistically significant? |
|---|---|
| *Woman reports of:* | |
| Physical argument in the last year (%) | Yes |
| Number of fights woman hit, shoved, or threw things at man | No |
| Was man ever cut, bruised, or seriously injured in an argument? | No |
| Number of fights man hit, shoved, or threw things at woman | No |
| Was woman ever cut, bruised, or seriously injured in an argument? | No |
| *Man reports of:* | |
| Physical argument in the last year (%) | No |
| Number of fights woman hit, shoved, or threw things at man | No |
| Was man ever cut, bruised, or seriously injured in an argument? | No |
| Number of fights man hit, shoved, or threw things at woman | No |
| Was woman ever cut, bruised, or seriously injured in an argument? | No |

the results of the analyses performed for reports of intimate partner violence using multivariate models, as depicted in Figure 6.1 (for a list of all other characteristics included in each best fitting model, see Table A3 in the Appendix).

The analysis of the measures of intimate partner violence that included individual-level and couple-level characteristics confirms the findings in Table 6.7. Women in Traditional couples were significantly less likely to report that they had a physical argument in the previous year than were women in other couples. This difference could reflect a lower frequency of physical arguments in these couples relative to others; that would be consistent with men's reports, though men's reports do not show significant class differences. However, it could also reflect an internalization of cultural norms around gendered violence that surround the stereotypical separate spheres household: women in a "traditional household" do not speak of physical arguments because that would imply that they are not performing their roles as wives appropriately and have to be reprimanded by their husbands. This line of victim-blaming argumentation is often used to explain why many women do not report intimate partner violence.

## Summary

Our argument is that housework can be seen as a proxy for power dynamics in a household. If we understand how housework is divided, we can gain insights into how couples make decisions and how spouses attempt to influence one another's behavior. In this chapter, we have investigated two key areas where spouses could exercise power over one another, both latent and overt power. The strongest evidence for the use of latent power was found in the struggle over labor-market participation in Ultra-Traditional couples, where women want to work more hours than they currently do and men want their wives to work even less. There is a substantial amount of internal consistency in the other four classes in their division of housework and their paid employment preferences for each spouse. The majority of couples in our sample prefer that each spouse have paid work hours that reflect a desire to support their division of labor at home. Rather than a power struggle over pulling and pushing spouses out of or into the labor market, our findings note that the power dynamics driving the determination of the division of housework are also structuring spouses' preferred work hours for themselves and their partners.

Conflict resolution techniques also reflect the negotiation of power in couples. We have some evidence that Ultra-Traditional couples are navigating a challenging cultural space given that their division of labor is more extremely gender-typed than any other class. This experience of being so different from others and from the cultural norm may explain not only the increased number of disagreements, but also the women's silencing of themselves during disagreements. Reports of physical violence among couples in the Ultra-Traditional class also reflect a gendered power dynamic. That men report no physical violence being initiated by women and very little by them despite having reported some physical disagreements is consistent with the notion that Ultra-Traditional men would not admit that their wives could physically attack and/or injure them. Injuries were exactly equally distributed as reported by men in the Ultra-Traditional class, suggesting that they thought that any physical argument injured each spouse equally.

Men in the Traditional and Egalitarian classes report approximately the same number of physical arguments and the same number as initiated by either women or men, but men in the Traditional class report equal injuries, as do Ultra-Traditional men. Men in the Egalitarian class report being injured more frequently. Men in both classes seem to be navigating power dynamics in ways that are consistent with the literature. Like men in the Ultra-Traditional class, men in the Traditional class report that when there are injuries, both women and men are injured. However, men in the Egalitarian class are either (1) experiencing women's equalizing of power in their relationships through being the recipient of a physical injury in an argument or (2) feeling as though they should report an injury when it has occurred. That women's and men's reports of men's injuries are generally consistent in all classes other than the Egalitarian class (excluding the small numbers in the Egalitarian High Workload class) does suggest that men in the Egalitarian class are potentially being injured at a higher rate.

Alternatively, this could be evidence of gender-deviance neutralization, where men respond in an overly masculine way when in a situation that may be female-typed. That is, if women in the Egalitarian class are more likely to initiate physical violence, men may respond with greater force than in other couples in order to not be seen as a victim. Given the relatively small number of couples reporting intimate partner violence and that our multivariate models had difficulty differentiating between groups, these differences should be interpreted as an indication that further investigation is warranted into the extent to which the findings reflect differences across housework classes.

Overall, then, there is some support for viewing the division of housework within couples as a proxy for household power dynamics. Men and women exert latent power in structuring how much time in the labor market their spouse may want to spend. Both men and women also exert overt power through the use of verbal disagreements and physical violence, as evidenced among couples in the Ultra-Traditional and Egalitarian classes. Again, while not a deterministic model, our classification of couples by housework performance does provide insights into the power dynamics among U.S. couples in the late 1980s.

Chapters 4–6 have focused on a snapshot: an investigation of the division of labor and its correlates and consequences at one point in time in a couple's life. Another way to understand the power dynamics in a couple is to examine whether and how their behavior changes over time. Our investigation into this process of change over time begins in Chapter 7, where we present an analysis of change in class membership over time. We examine the characteristics of couples whose class is stable across five years and of those who become either more traditional or more egalitarian in their division of labor.

# 7

# Stability and change in class membership over time

## Introduction

Chapters 5 and 6 demonstrated how class membership based upon couples' division of housework was connected to individual- and couple-level characteristics. Chapter 5 documented the general characteristics of the five classes. Housework performance, as measured by class membership, reflected how power was negotiated within the household. We saw differences across the five classes in spouses' relationships to the labor market, their gender attitudes, and demographic characteristics like race/ethnicity and religious affiliation. Chapter 6 provided an empirical assessment of our key claim that housework performance can be seen as a proxy for household power dynamics. We found that there is some support for this claim as men in the Ultra-Traditional couples and women in the Egalitarian High Workload couples seem to be exercising overt power. Additionally, both women and men seem to exert latent power in structuring their spouses' labor-market hours, and both women and men acquiesce to the exercise of this power. These insights regarding the associations between housework class and the possible utilization of power can be seen as evidence of the key claim of this book. Additional evidence to support this claim may be observed when examining couple class membership over time.

Housework performance as reported in survey data is a snapshot in time. Our arguments about power dynamics among U.S. couples are based on analysis of survey data collected from couples at one point in time. The question that follows next in this logic asks about the extent to which class membership is stable over time. As individuals age, they may (or may not) gain tenure in employment, seek more education, secure better jobs, have more children, and simply have more life experiences. These and similar events have the potential to either reinforce current power dynamics in the household and housework distribution or lead to a renegotiation. If our argument is sound—that housework performance is a proxy for power dynamics in a couple—then we should be able to discern changes in family dynamics over time as a result of power, in this case, as correlated with the typology of housework performance. To examine whether class membership changed over time, we performed latent trajectory analysis (for details, see the Appendix). In this chapter, we discuss the transitions in housework performance evidenced among the National Survey of Families and Households (NSFH) couples between Waves 1 and 2. First, we examine whether couples changed class membership over time. Did they become more traditional or more egalitarian in their housework division, or did they stay the same? Here, we document whether there are patterns in Wave 1 characteristics that are correlated with change in class membership over time. We then present the Wave 2 class membership patterns and examine the characteristics of couples as measured in Wave 1. Essentially, were there patterns in Wave 1 characteristics that are correlated with Wave 2 class membership?

Given the challenging cultural terrain for the couples at both ends of the housework distribution (the Ultra-Traditional and Egalitarian High Workload couples), we would expect some "regression to the mean" among the couples. That is, we would expect that couples would move out of the two most extreme classes (Ultra-Traditional and Egalitarian High Workload) because of the minimal supports for either class during the time period over which the data were collected (for more details on the cultural context surrounding families during Wave 1, see Chapter 3). If there were movements from either the Egalitarian or Egalitarian High Workload classes toward a more traditional division of labor, we would consider those changes as evidence of men using both overt and latent power to make the division of labor more favorable to themselves. The extent to which the Ultra-Traditional and Egalitarian High Workload couples maintain their class membership over time would be evidence of the pervasiveness of, respectively, men's and women's power within these couples. In general, however, we would expect transitions to follow resources, that is, evidence of latent or even overt power would be seen when individuals with, in particular, more economic resources were able to secure a more favorable division of labor for themselves.

Changes in the distribution of resources may be more likely in some classes, especially the Transitional Husbands, Egalitarian, and Egalitarian High Workload classes, as women would be better situated to accumulate resources that could yield greater power in the home. However, as the resource distribution in the Ultra-Traditional and Traditional couples was predicated on men's economic opportunities, they would be poised for relative changes should there be economic structural changes. Indeed, the recession of the early 1990s would have been an external factor that could have led to housework (and other) renegotiations. This relatively mild recession lasted about eight months and saw unemployment rates in the U.S. climb to 7.8 percent, with approximately 1.6 million jobs lost (Gardner, 1994). Any changes in housework over time need to be examined with all of these theoretical and cultural contexts in mind.

## Stability and change over time in class membership

Life experiences shape change in housework performance, but how much of the general distribution of tasks between spouses stays the same over time? Using latent trajectory analysis, we examine the stability and change of class membership from Wave 1 (1987/88) of the NSFH to Wave 2 (1992/94). There was remarkable movement across the groups. The percentages listed in Table 7.1 are the percentages of the overall sample that, for example, were Ultra-Traditional in both time periods (3.1 percent) or were Traditional in Wave 1 but became a member of the Transitional Husbands class in Wave 2 (0.6 percent).

While there was some consistency in class membership over time, the Egalitarian High Workload class gained significant membership, moving to the largest class in the sample, comprising 41.1 percent of the couples. The Ultra-Traditional class substantially reduced in size to only 7.7 percent of the sample. Indeed, there was a marked movement into a more egalitarian division of labor in the couples in the time between Waves 1 and 2.

Table 7.1: Stability and change in class membership over time

| Class membership in Wave 1 | Class membership in Wave 2 | | | | |
|---|---|---|---|---|---|
| | Ultra-Traditional | Traditional | Transitional Husbands | Egalitarian | Egalitarian High Workload |
| Ultra-Traditional | 3.1 | 0.8 | 0.1 | 4.8 | 1.8 |
| Traditional | 0.2 | 10.1 | 0.6 | 2.4 | 5.2 |
| Transitional Husbands | 2.1 | 1.1 | 1.7 | 10.2 | 2.8 |
| Egalitarian | 1.8 | 3.2 | 1.7 | 9.3 | 30.8 |
| Egalitarian High Workload | 0.5 | 1.6 | 2.2 | 1.3 | 0.4 |
| Percentage of overall sample | 7.7 | 16.8 | 6.3 | 28.1 | 41.1 |

## Characteristics defining stability and change over time in class membership

What characterized couples that changed class membership over time to become more egalitarian or more traditional in their division of labor? Which couples were more likely to stay in the same class? Latent trajectory analysis allows us to examine whether couples maintained their class membership between the two waves of the NSFH. In this section, we examine the individual and couple characteristics for three categories of couples: those who became more egalitarian in their division of labor over time; those who became more traditional; and those whose class membership stayed the same. We begin by examining demographic characteristics and then examine Wave 1 measures of the theoretical frameworks predicting housework as correlates of whether there was stability or change in housework class membership over time in the couples in our sample.

### Couple characteristics

Table 7.2 documents the characteristics of couples as measured in Wave 1 and whether they became more traditional, more egalitarian, or maintained their division of labor over time. The table entries represent a snapshot of the couple-level characteristics measured at Time 1. For example, among couples who became more traditional over time, 8.8 percent were cohabiting while 66.2 percent were in their first marriage, the average marital duration was 17.1 years, and the couples reported having 1.3 children at Wave 1. Surprisingly, those who were cohabiting represented a larger percentage of the group who become more traditional in their division of labor than they were in the groups that became more egalitarian or stayed the same. Perhaps as cohabiters' relationship durations grew, they became more similar to married couples and, as a result, developed a division of labor that was more gender-typed. Those in their first marriage represented less

**Table 7.2:** Change in class membership and Wave 1 couple characteristics

|  | Class membership became more traditional | Class membership became more egalitarian | Class membership stayed the same |
|---|---|---|---|
| Cohabiting (%) | 8.8 | 6.6 | 5.9 |
| First marriage (%) | 66.2 | 71.3 | 72.2 |
| Marital duration (years) | 17.1 | 17.3 | 15.9 |
| Number of children | 1.3 | 1.1 | 1.1 |

of the group who became more traditional over time than the groups who stayed the same or became more egalitarian. This may be due to the overwhelming representation of those in a first marriage in the two most traditional housework classes at Wave 1.

### Spousal demographic characteristics

While there was little association between religion and whether couples' division of labor was stable or changed over time, Table 7.3 does demonstrate that there were some differences in the racial composition of couples and class membership over time. Couples that became more traditional over time were a significantly more racially diverse group than were those who became more egalitarian or maintained their class membership across the two interviews. This is likely due to the increased likelihood of couples with non-white partners to be represented in the Egalitarian and Egalitarian

**Table 7.3:** Change in class membership and Wave 1 partner characteristics

| | Class membership became more traditional | Class membership became more egalitarian | Class membership stayed the same |
|---|---|---|---|
| **Woman's characteristics (%)** | | | |
| *Race* | | | |
| White | 83.1 | 91.2 | 89.0 |
| Black | 10.9 | 4.9 | 4.9 |
| Hispanic | 5.7 | 2.9 | 4.8 |
| Other race | 0.3 | 1.3 | 1.3 |
| *Religion* | | | |
| Protestant | 62.0 | 65.2 | 63.4 |
| Catholic | 27.1 | 22.0 | 27.6 |
| Other religion | 3.4 | 4.9 | 2.0 |
| No religion | 7.4 | 7.8 | 7.0 |
| **Man's characteristics (%)** | | | |
| *Race* | | | |
| White | 80.8 | 90.9 | 87.7 |
| Black | 11.5 | 5.4 | 5.5 |
| Hispanic | 6.9 | 3.3 | 5.0 |
| Other race | 0.9 | 0.4 | 1.8 |
| *Religion* | | | |
| Protestant | 57.5 | 60.0 | 59.6 |
| Catholic | 28.4 | 22.4 | 26.9 |
| Other religion | 2.9 | 2.1 | 1.3 |
| No religion | 10.1 | 12.3 | 10.4 |

High Workload classes in Wave 1. If those couples were going to change their class membership, the most likely change would be to become more traditional.

### Time availability

Table 7.4 demonstrates that there were generally no differences in actual or preferred labor-market hours for either women or men as measured in Wave 1 and the extent to which there was change or stability in housework class membership in Wave 2. Couples where men preferred to be working more were the most likely to become more egalitarian over time in their division of housework. This statistically significant difference can be seen as an expression of women's latent power as it could be due to women being able to convince their husbands to spend those hours on work in the home.

**Table 7.4:** Change in class membership and Wave 1 labor-market and preferred labor-market hours

|  | Class membership became more traditional | Class membership became more egalitarian | Class membership stayed the same |
|---|---|---|---|
| Woman's average weekly work hours | 23.0 | 22.5 | 24.2 |
| Man's average weekly work hours | 37.2 | 39.2 | 38.1 |
| Woman's preferred working hours | 22.7 | 20.5 | 22.1 |
| Difference between woman's preferred and actual working hours | −0.2 | 1.2 | 1.8 |
| Woman's preferred working hours for man | 33.4 | 33.2 | 32.1 |
| Difference between preferred and actual working hours for man as reported by woman | 3.8 | 6.0 | 5.5 |
| Man's preferred working hours | 34.3 | 34.2 | 35.2 |
| Difference between man's preferred and actual working hours | 2.4 | 5.0 | 2.2 |
| Man's preferred working hours for woman | 19.2 | 18.4 | 19.3 |
| Difference between preferred and actual working hours for woman as reported by man | 3.0 | 3.5 | 4.8 |

## Bargaining theory and absolute resources

There was some evidence for the connection between the absolute resources of the spouses in Wave 1 as possible measures of power and change in housework class membership over time. As Table 7.5 documents, couples who became more traditional in their class membership over time were significantly more likely to have women with low occupational prestige scores in Wave 1. It is likely that because the women were in low-prestige jobs, the couples could more easily become more gender-typical in their division of labor as the women's jobs did not afford them bargaining power within the couple. Couples who became more traditional also had men with relatively low incomes and thus significantly lower household incomes overall. As neither men's educational attainment nor occupational prestige in this group were significantly different than those of men in the couples that became more egalitarian or did not change class membership over time, we see these two related differences as possible examples of gender-deviance neutralization. Couples with men who were relatively low earners became more traditional in their division of housework to potentially neutralize men's unclear status as the breadwinner in the household. Finally, couples with older spouses were significantly more likely to become egalitarian over time.

Table 7.5: Change in class membership and Wave 1 absolute resources

|  | Class membership became more traditional | Class membership became more egalitarian | Class membership stayed the same |
|---|---|---|---|
| Woman's earnings ($) | 11,911 | 13,094 | 15,853 |
| Man's earnings ($) | 23,294 | 29,325 | 26,002 |
| Woman's occupational prestige | 3,945.9 | 4,446.8 | 4,328.2 |
| Man's occupational prestige | 4,104.0 | 4,312.6 | 4,182.2 |
| Woman's educational attainment | 13.0 | 13.4 | 13.3 |
| Man's educational attainment | 13.0 | 13.6 | 13.5 |
| Woman's age | 37.1 | 38.3 | 36.8 |
| Man's age | 39.7 | 40.6 | 38.9 |
| Household income ($) | 34,851 | 42,884 | 41,409 |

## Bargaining theory and relative resources

Couples where women had higher relative educational attainment at the first interview were more likely to change their class membership and become more egalitarian by the second interview. This change, documented in Table 7.6, provides evidence for housework as a measure of power within couples as women were able to use the bargaining power that accrues with higher levels of education to negotiate a more egalitarian division of housework over time. Further, couples where women had higher relative incomes were significantly more likely to maintain their class membership over time. Conversely, couples where women had lower relative incomes were more likely to change their class membership. Perhaps women with less earning power relative to their husbands were more likely to change their division of labor to meet their husbands' desires, an example of husbands' latent power.

**Table 7.6:** Change in class membership and Wave 1 relative resources

|  | Class membership became more traditional | Class membership became more egalitarian | Class membership stayed the same |
|---|---|---|---|
| Woman's relative income | 0.259 | 0.233 | 0.275 |
| Woman's relative occupational prestige | 1.216 | 1.220 | 1.248 |
| Woman's relative education | 1.021 | 1.104 | 1.020 |

## Gender ideology

Gender ideology at the first interview measured each partner's attitudes toward a traditionally gendered division of paid and unpaid work. Table 7.7 notes that there was no difference in the women's or men's overall gender ideology score at the first interview and whether the couples changed their housework class or stayed in the same class.

However, there were differences in *couple* gender ideology that are suggestive of the reciprocal relationship between ideology and housework. The majority of couples became more egalitarian in their division of housework, regardless of their ideology at Wave 1. Couples where the woman was egalitarian and the man was traditional were most likely to maintain their class membership; couples where both partners were traditional or the man was traditional and woman was

**Table 7.7:** Change in class membership and Wave 1 gender ideology

| | Class membership became more traditional | Class membership became more egalitarian | Class membership stayed the same |
|---|---|---|---|
| Woman's ideology score | 97.3 | 98.1 | 97.5 |
| Man's ideology score | 97.0 | 98.8 | 97.4 |
| Couple ideology distribution (% in class membership change category) | | | |
| Both traditional | 13.5 | 64.3 | 22.2 |
| Both transitional | 14.8 | 61.8 | 23.4 |
| Both egalitarian | 15.6 | 58.4 | 26.0 |
| Woman traditional/man transitional | 13.9 | 60.8 | 25.4 |
| Woman traditional/man egalitarian | 20.0 | 57.1 | 22.9 |
| Woman transitional/man traditional | 14.4 | 63.4 | 22.3 |
| Woman transitional/man egalitarian | 19.3 | 54.2 | 26.5 |
| Woman egalitarian/man traditional | 15.2 | 56.1 | 28.8 |
| Woman egalitarian/man transitional | 15.3 | 58.1 | 26.6 |

transitional were the least likely to maintain their class membership over time. Interestingly, the two types of couples most likely to become more traditional in their division of household labor over time were those where women held more traditional ideologies than did their spouses (woman traditional/man egalitarian and women transitional/man egalitarian). This change over time may be indicative of women attempting to reduce cognitive dissonance by aligning their household division of labor with their own beliefs. As a gender-typical division of labor is the path of least resistance and culturally most prevalent, even slightly more egalitarian husbands may find it easier to move toward a more traditional division of labor.

## Demographic characteristics of class membership in Wave 2

Similar to Chapters 5 and 6, we include here a description of the couples in their housework classes in the second wave based upon their individual- and couple-level characteristics. We begin with demographic characteristics. Table 7.8 presents the socio-demographic characteristics of couples by class membership in Wave 2.

At the second wave, we see divergence in the classes regarding whether the class is comprised of cohabiting couples, whether the marriage is a first marriage, and the length of marriage among those married. The couples in the Traditional class are significantly less

**Table 7.8:** Wave 2 class membership and couple characteristics

|  | Ultra-Traditional | Traditional | Transitional Husbands | Egalitarian | Egalitarian High Workload |
|---|---|---|---|---|---|
| Cohabiting (%) | 7.6 | 0.8 | 9.3 | 4.3 | 7.4 |
| First marriage (%) | 72.0 | 68.1 | 61.9 | 73.1 | 71.3 |
| Marital duration (years) | 17.5 | 15.9 | 14.9 | 17.7 | 17.6 |
| Number of children | 1.5 | 0.9 | 1.5 | 1.4 | 0.9 |

likely to be cohabiting than are the couples in the other classes. Surprisingly, the Ultra-Traditional and Egalitarian High Workload classes are remarkably similar in Wave 2. While the Egalitarian High Workload class was comprised of more cohabiting couples and those in a second or higher-order marriage at Wave 1, these characteristics are more likely to be found among couples in the Transitional Husbands class in Wave 2.

Table 7.9 presents information about where couples lived at Wave 1 and their class membership in Wave 2. There was little variation in geographic distribution by region at Wave 1 and class membership in Wave 2. One key difference was the increased likelihood of those living in the South and a concomitant decreased likelihood of those living in the West at Wave 1 to be a member of the Ultra-Traditional class at Wave 2 (relative to being in other classes). Those living in metropolitan areas at Wave 1 were significantly less likely to be in the Ultra-Traditional class in Wave 2.

Table 7.10 presents partner demographic characteristics as reflected across class membership in Wave 2. In contrast to Wave 1, the class with the greatest racial diversity in Wave 2 was the Transitional Husbands class. There was generally no substantial difference in class membership in Wave 2 by religious affiliation, though the Traditional

**Table 7.9:** Wave 2 class membership and geographic location

|  | Ultra-Traditional | Traditional | Transitional Husbands | Egalitarian | Egalitarian High Workload |
|---|---|---|---|---|---|
| **Region of the country (%)** |  |  |  |  |  |
| Northeast | 15.2 | 19.4 | 14.3 | 17.1 | 18.8 |
| North Central | 33.9 | 30.1 | 32.1 | 33.2 | 32.8 |
| South | 36.8 | 29.5 | 30.0 | 29.4 | 31.7 |
| West | 14.0 | 21.0 | 23.6 | 20.3 | 16.7 |
| Live in metropolitan area (%) | 61.4 | 78.2 | 75.7 | 67.9 | 73.4 |

**Table 7.10:** Wave 2 class membership and partner demographic characteristics

| | Ultra-Traditional | Traditional | Transitional Husbands | Egalitarian | Egalitarian High Workload |
|---|---|---|---|---|---|
| **Woman's characteristics (%)** | | | | | |
| *Race* | | | | | |
| White | 82.4 | 91.7 | 76.8 | 89.1 | 91.3 |
| Black | 8.8 | 5.1 | 14.5 | 5.1 | 4.8 |
| Hispanic | 8.8 | 2.4 | 8.0 | 4.0 | 2.6 |
| Other race | 0 | 0.8 | 0.7 | 1.1 | 1.2 |
| *Religion* | | | | | |
| Protestant | 62.0 | 57.4 | 63.3 | 70.4 | 63.5 |
| Catholic | 28.7 | 32.2 | 24.5 | 21.8 | 21.7 |
| Other religion | 3.5 | 2.1 | 4.3 | 2.1 | 6.1 |
| No religion | 5.8 | 8.3 | 7.9 | 5.7 | 8.8 |
| **Man's characteristics (%)** | | | | | |
| *Race* | | | | | |
| White | 84.1 | 89.3 | 72.5 | 88.9 | 91.2 |
| Black | 9.4 | 6.4 | 10.9 | 5.4 | 5.1 |
| Hispanic | 6.5 | 2.9 | 10.9 | 4.6 | 3.2 |
| Other race | 0 | 1.3 | 2.2 | 1.0 | 0.4 |
| *Religion* | | | | | |
| Protestant | 59.8 | 54.7 | 58.4 | 61.8 | 60.0 |
| Catholic | 26.6 | 28.7 | 28.5 | 23.7 | 22.3 |
| Other religion | 3.0 | 1.6 | 2.2 | 1.5 | 2.4 |
| No religion | 9.5 | 13.7 | 8.8 | 11.6 | 11.3 |

class was significantly more likely to include couples where the wife was Catholic than were the other classes.

## Wave 1 measures of theoretical frameworks explaining housework and Wave 2 class membership

### Time availability

Table 7.11 examines the Wave 2 class membership of couples based upon measures of the time availability theoretical framework. Labor-market hours for both spouses are included in this table, as are the measures of each spouse's preferred labor-market hours for themselves and their spouse. While there is little variation in Wave 2 class membership based upon Wave 1 working hours for men (despite the finding that men in the Wave 2 Egalitarian High Workload class worked significantly more hours in Wave 1 than did men in the Wave 2 Traditional class), there is substantial variability for women's working hours. Surprisingly, women with very low working hours in Wave 1 were equally likely to be in couples in the Ultra-Traditional or Egalitarian classes in Wave 2, and significantly less likely to be in one of the other three classes. Additionally, women in the Ultra-Traditional and Egalitarian classes in Wave 2 were the only women who wanted to work fewer hours at Wave 1, which is another significant difference. Women in the Ultra-Traditional and Egalitarian High Workload classes in Wave 2 reported wanting their spouses to work more hours in the labor market than they actually were in Wave 1. Women who were

**Table 7.11:** Wave 2 class membership and Wave 1 actual and preferred labor-market hours

|  | Ultra-Traditional | Traditional | Transitional Husbands | Egalitarian | Egalitarian High Workload |
|---|---|---|---|---|---|
| Woman's average weekly work hours | 14.3 | 28.7 | 25.0 | 15.6 | 25.1 |
| Man's average weekly work hours | 36.9 | 33.7 | 34.3 | 36.3 | 38.6 |
| Woman's preferred working hours | 20.5 | 23.5 | 23.1 | 19.1 | 21.7 |
| Difference between woman's preferred and actual working hours | −3.1 | 3.2 | 1.2 | −2.3 | 3.3 |
| Woman's preferred working hours for man | 31.9 | 33.1 | 32.2 | 32.6 | 33.4 |
| Difference between preferred and actual working hours for man as reported by woman | 6.0 | 2.2 | −1.3 | 3.4 | 5.4 |
| Man's preferred working hours | 32.3 | 34.2 | 36.4 | 35.1 | 34.2 |
| Difference between man's preferred and actual working hours | 5.2 | 3.9 | 2.4 | 5.7 | 6.4 |
| Man's preferred working hours for woman | 16.9 | 20.7 | 19.7 | 16.7 | 19.6 |
| Difference between preferred and actual working hours for woman as reported by man | 0.6 | 6.0 | 4.5 | 0.3 | 5.6 |

in the Transitional Husbands class in Wave 2 reported wanting their husbands to work fewer hours when interviewed in Wave 1.

Regardless of their housework class membership in Wave 2, men reported approximately the same number of preferred working hours when interviewed in Wave 1. In general, men in all of the classes at Wave 2 reported wanting to work substantially more hours than they actually were when interviewed in Wave 1, with men in the Transitional Husbands class reporting the greatest similarity between their actual and preferred working hours.

## Bargaining theory and absolute resources

We next examine the resource-based characteristics of spouses when interviewed at Wave 1 as represented in class membership in Wave 2. As shown in Table 7.12, women in the Ultra-Traditional class at the second interview had the lowest absolute income at the first interview; women in the Transitional Husbands and Egalitarian High Workload classes at the second interview had reported more than twice the income of women in the Ultra-Traditional class, which are all statistically significant differences. Men's incomes at the first interview were quite similar across the housework classes at Wave 2, though Egalitarian High Workload men did report slightly (but significantly) higher incomes than other men at the first interview. This significant difference is also reflected in overall household income.

**Table 7.12:** Wave 2 class membership and Wave 1 absolute resources

|  | Ultra-Traditional | Traditional | Transitional Husbands | Egalitarian | Egalitarian High Workload |
|---|---|---|---|---|---|
| Woman's earnings ($) | 7,586 | 15,431 | 14,146 | 11,733 | 14,796 |
| Man's earnings ($) | 22,928 | 26,327 | 20,783 | 27,475 | 30,014 |
| Woman's occupational prestige | 3,701 | 4,495 | 4,212 | 4,053 | 4,559 |
| Man's occupational prestige | 3,530 | 4,609 | 3,957 | 4,093 | 4,430 |
| Woman's educational attainment | 12.5 | 13.7 | 12.9 | 12.9 | 13.6 |
| Man's educational attainment | 12.6 | 14.0 | 12.7 | 13.1 | 13.8 |
| Woman's age | 37.7 | 36.7 | 35.3 | 38.2 | 38.3 |
| Man's age | 40.1 | 39.3 | 38.1 | 40.3 | 40.4 |
| Household income ($) | 28,462 | 42,378 | 32,422 | 39,718 | 45,526 |

Other statistically significant differences across the Wave 2 classes in the absolute resources measured in Wave 1 were in both spouse's occupational prestige and educational attainment. Couples in the Ultra-Traditional class at the second interview reported having the lowest occupational prestige of all couples during the first interview. Couples in the Traditional and Egalitarian High Workload classes at Wave 2 had the highest reported educational attainment during the first interview.

### Bargaining theory and relative resources

As bargaining theory argues that relative resources are crucial for determining the division of household labor, Table 7.13 examines couples' relative resources at the first interview and their class membership at Wave 2. While there is little variation across classes at the second interview in relative educational attainment as measured at the first interview, couples that reported the lowest relative incomes for wives at the first interview were significantly more likely to be in the Ultra-Traditional and Egalitarian classes at Wave 2. The findings for Ultra-Traditional women are consistent with what would be expected if men were exerting power over their wives' behavior in between the two time periods. Couples where women have lower relative income would see women doing more housework, as is the case for Ultra-Traditional class couples. However, this explanation does little to account for the anomalous finding of the Egalitarian couples. Perhaps (as we note later) this is due to the fact that almost half of Egalitarian couples have one member who holds traditional gender attitudes.

**Table 7.13:** Wave 2 class membership and Wave 1 relative resources

|  | Ultra-Traditional | Traditional | Transitional Husbands | Egalitarian | Egalitarian High Workload |
|---|---|---|---|---|---|
| Wife's relative income | 0.17 | 0.31 | 0.30 | 0.18 | 0.27 |
| Wife's relative occupational prestige | 1.28 | 1.22 | 1.35 | 1.18 | 1.23 |
| Wife's relative education | 1.02 | 1.01 | 1.06 | 1.02 | 1.01 |

### Gender ideology

There is some variation in the distribution of couples across housework class membership at the second interview based upon gender ideology (measured at the individual and couple level) at the first interview. Table 7.14 demonstrates similarity in the Ultra-Traditional and Egalitarian classes in individual spouse gender ideology, mirroring what we saw in the relationship between Wave 1 relative income and Wave 2 class membership. Couples in the Ultra-Traditional and Egalitarian classes at the second interview were comprised of the women and men who held the most gender-traditional attitudes at the first interview; indeed, they were statistically significantly distinct from the other three classes. We can certainly see how individuals, and couples, with gender-traditional attitudes at Wave 1 were more likely to be in the Ultra-Traditional class at Wave 2; this may be an effort to reduce cognitive dissonance between attitudes and behaviors. Couples who were in the Egalitarian class at Wave 2 had a relatively high likelihood of one partner having been traditional with the other being egalitarian or transitional at the first interview. Perhaps these couples represent an exertion of latent power from both women and men to encourage their partner to become more of an equal partner in the housework.

**Table 7.14:** Wave 2 class membership and Wave 1 gender ideology

| | Ultra-Traditional | Traditional | Transitional Husbands | Egalitarian | Egalitarian High Workload |
|---|---|---|---|---|---|
| Woman's ideology score | 102.1 | 93.6 | 97.9 | 100.4 | 97.0 |
| Man's ideology score | 103.7 | 93.5 | 93.4 | 101.5 | 97.6 |
| **Couple ideology distribution (%)** | | | | | |
| Both traditional | 22.4 | 8.5 | 26.9 | 18.9 | 14.6 |
| Both transitional | 21.2 | 15.2 | 8.7 | 19.2 | 18.1 |
| Both egalitarian | 7.1 | 20.3 | 20.6 | 10.5 | 20.4 |
| Woman traditional/ man transitional | 9.0 | 7.6 | 11.1 | 11.8 | 10.0 |
| Woman traditional/ man egalitarian | 6.4 | 2.0 | 6.3 | 2.9 | 3.3 |
| Woman transitional/ man traditional | 13.5 | 9.0 | 4.8 | 11.7 | 8.8 |
| Woman transitional/ man egalitarian | 7.1 | 14.6 | 18.3 | 11.1 | 11.5 |
| Woman egalitarian/ man traditional | 6.4 | 2.3 | 4.0 | 2.7 | 3.2 |
| Woman egalitarian/ man transitional | 7.1 | 12.4 | 11.9 | 11.1 | 10.2 |

## Predicting Wave 2 class membership

The previous analyses have examined differences in Wave 2 class membership one characteristic at a time. Table 7.15 presents the results of the best fitting statistical model that includes multiple characteristics, or predictors, simultaneously. To do this, we employ multinomial logistic regression using Traditional class membership as the reference category, just as we did in Chapter 5 when we predicted initial class membership. As in Chapter 5, we present the odds ratios resulting from our analysis. As a reminder, odds ratios are interpreted here as the odds that a couple will be classified as the specific class (for example, Ultra-Traditional) versus being classified as Traditional given a change in a particular predictor (for example, an increase in the man's income), net the effects of all of the other characteristics included in the model. If the odds ratio is greater than 1, an increase in the predictor increases the likelihood of being in the specific class relative to the Traditional class. If the odds ratio is less than 1, an increase in the predictor decreases the likelihood of being in the specific class relative to the Traditional class.

**Table 7.15:** Predicting Wave 2 class membership

| Characteristic | Ultra-Traditional (versus Traditional) | Transitional Husbands (versus Traditional) | Egalitarian (versus Traditional) | Egalitarian High Workload (versus Traditional) |
|---|---|---|---|---|
| *Time availability* | | | | |
| Woman's average weekly work hours | 1.001 | 1.000 | 0.993* | 1.006 |
| *Absolute resources* | | | | |
| Man's educational attainment | 0.905* | 0.861* | 0.935* | 0.997 |
| Man's earnings | 0.999* | 0.999* | 1.000 | 1.000 |
| *Gender Ideology* | | | | |
| Man's ideology score | 1.029* | 0.988 | 1.018* | 1.013* |
| *Couple characteristic* | | | | |
| Number of children | 1.271* | 1.396* | 1.117* | 1.000 |
| *Wave 1 class membership* | | | | |
| Ultra-Traditional | 7.603* | 3.461* | 4.765* | 0.766 |
| Transitional Husbands | 0.352* | 0.611 | 0.307* | 0.174* |
| Egalitarian | 0.273* | 0.887 | 0.302* | 0.139* |
| Egalitarian High Workload | 0.434 | 2.158* | 0.224* | 0.051* |

Note: $*p < .05$.

The best fitting statistical model predicting Wave 2 class membership includes measures of time availability, absolute resources, and gender ideology, as well as one couple-level demographic characteristic alongside Wave 1 class membership. The measures included are all statistically significant predictors of differentiating across the housework classes at Wave 2. As in Chapter 5, we have chosen to present the odds relative to the Traditional class. The model presented here confirms some of the descriptive analysis presented earlier in the chapter, net of the longitudinal influence of Wave 1 class membership. Those couples classified as Ultra-Traditional are characterized by men with lower educational attainment and earnings who hold more "traditional" gender ideologies, and couples with more children than are couples classified as Traditional. Those classified as Transitional Husbands are also characterized by men with lower educational attainment and earnings (but who hold similar gender ideologies), and couples with more children than are couples classified as Traditional. Those classified as Egalitarian are characterized by women who work fewer hours, men with lower educational attainment who hold more "traditional" gender ideologies, and couples with more children than are couples classified as Traditional. Finally, couples classified as Egalitarian High Workload are characterized by men holding more "traditional" gender ideologies than are couples classified as Traditional.

Consistent with Table 7.1, Table 7.15 demonstrates the mobility in class membership from Wave 1 to Wave 2, net of measures of time availability, men's resources and gender ideology, and number of children. In comparing Table 7.1 to 7.15, the key differences in the likelihood of living in a particular housework class is based on the distribution of individual and couple characteristics across the classes. The movement between classes demonstrated in Table 7.1 is explained, in part, by the variation in and changes over time in the couples' demographic characteristics. These two tables simultaneously provide support for the interconnected nature of the task distribution across the five classes and the measures of the main theoretical frameworks described in Chapter 2.

## Summary

This chapter has examined the extent to which couples in the five housework classes maintained their division of labor over time or modified their sharing of the housework tasks. Consistent with previous scholarship on housework using more recent data (for example, Nitsche and Grunow, 2016), our analysis demonstrated that the division of housework shifted among the majority of couples over time. Couples were more likely to change class membership than to stay the same. There was movement in both directions, with couples becoming both more traditional and more egalitarian. It is not surprising to see couples becoming more traditional in their division of housework over time as it is harder to maintain a non-traditional division of labor given that the structure of most workplaces still presumes a gender-typed division of household responsibilities. For the Egalitarian High Workload individuals in particular, maintaining the high volume of housework (as documented in Chapter 4) over the five-year time period would be especially challenging.

Couples changing their division of housework, as documented by their transitions in class membership, also demonstrates some evidence of the use of power among the couples (for example, couples who became more traditional in their class membership over time were more likely to have women with low occupational prestige scores and relative incomes in Wave 1). These changes provide additional support for our claim that the distribution of housework can be seen as a proxy for power dynamics within households. Again, while not deterministic, the power relationships that existed within couples at Time 1 played out in the extent to which partners were able to mobilize resources and change the division of labor (and thereby change or maintain class membership) over time. The use of latent power is also evident among these couples in the extent to which couples' housework time is connected to the activation of resources and the reduction of cognitive dissonance. This can be seen among couples with men who were relatively low earners becoming more traditional in their division of labor in an attempt to neutralize their unclear status as breadwinners, and with women who held more traditional ideologies than did their spouses becoming more traditional in their division of housework in order to align their division of labor to their beliefs.

This chapter has examined the similarity and differences in couples' division of housework tasks over a five-year time period. Chapter 8 will address the questions of whether changes in spouses' characteristics connected with power, such as income, occupational prestige, and work hours, are connected with changes in housework class membership.

# 8

# Housework over
# the family life course

## Introduction

To highlight the value of our approach of using housework to understand power in families, in this chapter, we seek evidence of the usage of overt/hidden and latent power across the family life course of a selection of heterosexual couples. We examine predictions about how shifts in the power dynamics within the household (measured through changes in housework performance and documented via our typology) are connected to economic shifts. Specifically, we examine whether changes in specific characteristics associated with power in the public sphere between Waves 1 and 2 of the National Survey of Families and Households (NSFH) are patterned across changes in class membership over time.

Studying connections between measures of women's and men's economic characteristics at two time points and the amount that they change over time allows for a clear examination of the interplay of power dynamics within couples. While we recognize that external factors also shape labor-market experiences for both women and men, transitions in behaviors and resources that are correlated with the distribution of housework are likely to be consistently influenced by those external forces. Thus, we expect to see some patterning of shifts in work hours, absolute and relative incomes, and absolute and relative occupational prestige in the time period between Waves 1 and 2 that somewhat correspond to the couples' class membership in Time 1, the direction of change (if any) in their division of housework tasks, and their resulting housework class membership at Wave 2. In this chapter, therefore, we build on the argumentation and analysis in Chapter 7 to document the extent to which power may be evidenced across the classes. We expect to see evidence of the exercise of latent or hidden power such that women's and men's changes in labor-market hours (as well as other characteristics that are afforded power in the public sphere) would reflect their Wave 1 division of housework. For example, we would expect to find women in the Ultra-Traditional and Traditional classes to be more likely to reduce their working hours as an example of men's latent or hidden (or possibly overt) power. Similarly, we would expect Egalitarian High Workload men to transition to be more like their partners in work hours and income.

## Factors affecting change over time

First, we examine the effects of power as evidenced by housework performance by examining whether Time 1 class membership is correlated with changes in spouses' connection to the labor market over time. If class membership is representative of power, there should be differences evident in spousal behavior over time due to class membership, for example, a change in labor-market hours, relative earnings, or occupational prestige. We present this analysis in Table 8.1. In addition to the descriptive results presented in Table 8.1, Table 8.2 reports the results of path analysis models, structured as depicted in Figure 8.1. We regress each change in individual-level resources on class membership in Wave 1 as well as other individual-

**Table 8.1:** Wave 1 class membership and changes in resources

|  | Ultra-Traditional | Traditional | Transitional Husbands | Egalitarian | Egalitarian High Workload |
|---|---|---|---|---|---|
| Change in woman's average weekly work hours | 0.108 | −4.462 | 5.725 | −1.637 | −2.836 |
| Change in man's average weekly work hours | −5.052 | 2.345 | −2.859 | −2.410 | −1.970 |
| Change in woman's earnings ($) | 559 | 3,443 | 2,874 | 975 | 3,654 |
| Change in man's earnings ($) | −194 | 6,742 | 2,517 | 4,461 | 3,842 |
| Change in woman's relative income | 11.6 | 6.3 | 13.3 | 8.5 | 8.6 |
| Change in woman's occupational prestige | −658 | −592 | −8 | −495 | 120 |
| Change in man's occupational prestige | 150 | −1,018 | −284 | −593 | 88 |
| Change in woman's relative occupational prestige | −15.4 | 3.8 | −10.4 | −13.9 | −18.5 |

**Figure 8.1:** Multivariate modeling strategy for changes in individual-level resources

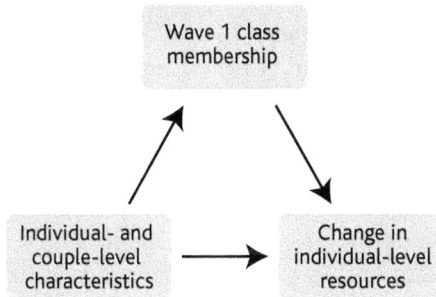

Wave 1 class membership

Individual- and couple-level characteristics → Change in individual-level resources

**Table 8.2:** Results of multivariate models predicting changes in resources

| Resource | Effect of Wave 1 class membership statistically significant? |
| --- | --- |
| Change in woman's average weekly work hours | No |
| Change in man's average weekly work hours | Yes |
| Change in woman's earnings ($) | No |
| Change in man's earnings ($) | No |
| Change in woman's relative income (%) | Yes |
| Change in woman's occupational prestige | No |
| Change in man's occupational prestige | No |
| Change in woman's relative occupational prestige (%) | No |

level and couple-level characteristics simultaneously (for more details on these statistical models, see the Appendix).

Consistent with earlier findings, we find evidence of couples shifting behaviors as part of their social exchange in the relationship. As shown in Table 8.1, couples who were in the Egalitarian and Egalitarian High Workload classes at Wave 1 saw statistically significant reductions in paid work hours for both men and women over time. That men in the Egalitarian class reported a greater reduction in hours than did women is suggestive of women's ability to encourage men to focus less on the labor market because of their commitment to responsibilities at home (that these men were ideologically inclined, as noted in Chapter 5, likely meant that the women had to exert relatively little power to encourage this change). Women in the Egalitarian High Workload class reduced their work hours more than men did in this class, potentially responding to the ideological pressure exerted by the men in this class, who were the most ideologically egalitarian of all men (as noted in Chapter 5).

The shift in labor-market time for the couples in the Egalitarian and Egalitarian High Workload classes is remarkable, in part, because of the increase in income experienced by the individuals in those couples. The reduction in labor-market time for men in the Egalitarian class occurred as men were reporting substantial increases in income, though their occupational prestige declined slightly (as did women's within the Egalitarian class). Both partners in Egalitarian High Workload couples experienced income increases between Wave 1 and Wave 2, and their occupational prestige scores remained largely constant. The overall changes in the relationship to the labor market through work hours, income, and occupational prestige for couples in the Egalitarian and Egalitarian High Workload classes suggest that the partners in these couples were able to secure more lucrative but flexible positions that could support their domestic responsibilities during the time between the interviews at Wave 1 and Wave 2.

Couples in the Traditional and Transitional Husbands classes also reflect changes in individual-level resources that are consistent with their modifying behavior over time in response to the power dynamics in the household reflected in the division of housework. Couples in the Transitional Husbands class saw a convergence of work hours and income between partners. While women in the Transitional Husbands class increased their work hours, their income increased approximately the same amount as did men's (who decreased their working hours). The virtual lack of change in occupational prestige for both spouses in this class suggests that the women were able to exert some power in these couples to secure greater labor-market participation for themselves and labor-market participation from their spouses that was more consistent with their domestic responsibilities.

Couples in the Traditional class reflect men's ability to secure a stronger position as the breadwinner in their household, further facilitating their disengagement from domestic responsibilities and the performance of housework tasks by the women. These couples saw significantly increased working hours among men and significantly decreased working hours among women. The increase in men's working hours was accompanied by a substantial increase in income despite a remarkable decline in occupational prestige. The jobs that men were working may have been less prestigious and required more time at work but were more lucrative. Women's income increased despite their decreased working hours and reduction in occupational prestige.[1]

Couples in the Ultra-Traditional class generally maintained their public–private sphere split from Wave 1 to Wave 2 as men were able to maintain a labor-market advantage (despite working fewer hours in Wave 2, they maintained a 15-hour advantage, as noted in Chapter 9). The stability in women's work hours and income and the reduction of women's occupational prestige reflect the ability of men in the Ultra-Traditional class to maintain their own connection to the labor market while securing women's connection to domestic work. That both women and men in this class held the most traditional gender ideologies (as noted in Chapter 5) likely meant that little power had to be exerted in order to maintain this division of responsibilities.

The descriptive findings find additional support in Table 8.2 in that Wave 1 class membership was a statistically significant predictor of changes in two resources—change in men's work hours and change in women's relative income—between Wave 1 and Wave 2 once other factors were included in the analysis. Symbolically, these two findings are important as they solidify the social and cultural value placed on both time and money. The performance of cultural norms supporting hegemonic masculinity would lead couples to encourage men to spend more time outside of the home in the labor force, especially if spouses want men to be identifiable as "traditional." That Ultra-Traditional men reduced their time in the labor force does not undermine this argument as they continued to maintain their labor-market advantage despite the reduction of hours. Increases in women's relative income were significantly smaller among the classes where women's roles relative to their husbands were more easily defined given the cultural climate of the times, as described in Chapter 3.

## Connecting class membership change with changes in resources

Next, we examine whether changes in the measures of spouses' individual-level resources that characterize their relationships with the labor market are patterned across the changes in class membership over time. Table 8.3 highlights the complicated nature of the lives of the couples that we are studying. Across the board, occupational prestige declined among both women and men, regardless of whether they maintained their class membership or became more traditional or more egalitarian in their division of labor. However, the decline was more pronounced among couples whose class membership reflected a more egalitarian division of labor in Wave 2. Coupled with the general flatness of work hours and increased income for both spouses but especially men, this suggests that couples whose division of labor became more egalitarian were able to facilitate a more egalitarian

**Table 8.3:** Change in class membership and changes in resources

| | Class membership became more traditional | Class membership became more egalitarian | Class membership stayed the same |
|---|---|---|---|
| Change in woman's average weekly work hours | 0.959 | −0.421 | −2.612 |
| Change in man's average weekly work hours | −4.151 | −1.2 | −2.002 |
| Change in woman's earnings ($) | 3,063 | 2,698 | −583 |
| Change in man's earnings ($) | 2,985 | 4,260 | 4,172 |
| Change in woman's relative income (%) | 12.1 | 9.4 | −6.7 |
| Change in woman's occupational prestige | −77 | −514 | −344 |
| Change in man's occupational prestige | −147 | −674 | −323 |
| Change in woman's relative occupational prestige (%) | −11.8 | −10.3 | −7.8 |

division of labor through a shift in their collective relationship to the labor market.

Couples who moved to a more traditional division of labor between Waves 1 and 2 did so as their occupational prestige was largely unchanged, women earned substantially more income, and men saw a significant reduction in their work hours. This change over time—where women earned more income and men worked less, yet the couples became more traditional in their division of labor—is a clear example of gender-deviance neutralization as a dynamic process (Greenstein, 2000). Both partners seem to be responding to a change in one another's behaviors in the public sphere (men working less and women earning more), and thus to neutralize the gender-atypical behavior in the public sphere, become more gender-typical in the private sphere.

Among the couples whose class membership stayed the same, the changes to hours worked and occupational prestige for the two partners were quite similar. The change in individual occupational prestige and subsequent reduced relative occupational prestige for women in couples whose class membership stayed the same between Wave 1 and Wave 2 are indicative of the fact that at Wave 1, the relative occupational prestige of those women was quite high (see Table 7.6). Among these couples (and not those couples whose class membership changed), women's incomes were basically flat but men's incomes increased. Taken together, these findings suggest that maintaining the status quo in the division of labor reflected responsiveness to the labor market by both spouses, but also reflected a reduction of women's relative earning power in the home.

As before, the findings in Table 8.3 are descriptive in nature, examining whether there were differences in the patterns of how couples changed housework class membership from Wave 1 to Wave 2 given specific changes in individual-level resources from Wave 1 to Wave 2. As with previous findings, we also performed multivariate analyses to predict whether couples changed class membership over time, using the modeling structure depicted in Figure 8.2. As individual-level and couple-level characteristics could directly influence class membership change, as well as indirectly through changes in resources over time, our multivariate models take into consideration all of these factors simultaneously. Table 8.4 reports the results of our multivariate path analysis models. We regress class membership change on the individual-level resources one at a time while simultaneously including other individual-level and couple-level characteristics (for more details on these statistical models, see the Appendix).

**Figure 8.2:** Multivariate modeling strategy for changes in housework class

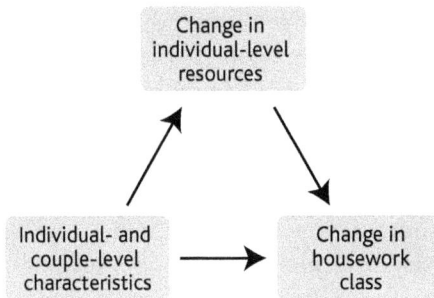

**Table 8.4:** Results of multivariate models predicting changes in housework class membership

| Resource | Effect of resource statistically significant? |
|---|:---:|
| Change in woman's average weekly work hours | No |
| Change in man's average weekly work hours | Yes |
| Change in woman's earnings ($) | Yes |
| Change in man's earnings ($) | No |
| Change in woman's relative income (%) | No |
| Change in woman's occupational prestige | No |
| Change in man's occupational prestige | Yes |
| Change in woman's relative occupational prestige (%) | No |

Few resource changes from Wave 1 to Wave 2 were significantly associated with class membership change, net of other individual-level and couple-level resources. Only the change in men's average weekly work hours, women's earnings, and men's occupational prestige were associated with class membership change. This is consistent with our argument that the use of resources is a gendered phenomenon reflecting the power dynamics within couples. Importantly, the resource held by women that was significantly associated with class membership change was women's changes in earnings, while changes in men's work hours and occupational prestige were significantly associated with class membership change. As noted earlier, the finding that, net of other characteristics, women's earnings increases seem to push couples toward becoming more traditional in their division of housework is evidence of gender-deviance neutralization. Given cultural norms around masculinity and femininity as tied to housework and paid labor, men may perform less in order to be seen as more masculine, also using their latent power to encourage their spouses to do more housework. Women may do more housework when they earn more money over time in order to maintain their own self-perception as appropriately gendered women. What is key is that it was women's income that was their only significant resource change that was associated with class membership change, reinforcing the renegotiation of the symbolic and material connections between financial resources and housework that was occurring when these data were collected.

The two resource changes among men that were significant predictors of class membership change, net of other characteristics, further demonstrate how resource use reflects power dynamics in households. Increases in men's work hours seemed to lead couples to becoming more traditional in their division of housework while a reduction in men's occupational prestige was significantly associated with couples becoming more egalitarian over time, net of other characteristics. Symbolically, that these were the two resources significantly associated with class membership change is important. Hours worked in the labor market reflect time not spent at home, and lower-prestige jobs may impact how others view the man's social status. Both of these characteristics are easily viewed and evaluated by those outside of the household, suggesting that the reason that changes in these resources are associated with changes in housework class is because of how they reflect on men's performance of hegemonic masculinity.

## Changes in resources and resulting class membership

In the previous sections, we examined how changes in resources were correlated with Wave 1 class membership and whether housework class membership changed from Wave 1 to Wave 2. In this section, we look at the correlation between changes in resources and Wave 2 class membership. While the analysis in Chapter 7 documented the characteristics of the couples in each of the Wave 2 classes based on measures of resources at Wave 1 (see Tables 7.12, 7.13, and 7.14), Table 8.5 documents the average level of change from Wave 1 to Wave 2 in the key measures of attachment to the labor market and resources within each Wave 2 housework class category. Further, we performed path analysis, as depicted in Figure 8.3, in order to use multivariate models to predict Wave 2 class. We included each measure of resource change independently along with other individual-level and couple-level resources as predictors of Wave 2 class. The results of these models are presented in Table 8.6 (for more details on the statistical models, see the Appendix).

Men in all Wave 2 classes reported working fewer hours in the second interview than they did in the first, but the reduction was

Table 8.5: Wave 2 class membership and changes in resources from Wave 1 to Wave 2

| | Ultra-Traditional | Traditional | Transitional Husbands | Egalitarian | Egalitarian High Workload |
|---|---|---|---|---|---|
| Change in woman's average weekly work hours | −3.104 | 1.743 | 0.219 | −1.561 | −0.924 |
| Change in man's average weekly work hours | −2.006 | −3.129 | −2.259 | −2.411 | −0.870 |
| Change in woman's earnings ($) | −896 | 4,892 | 2,726 | −2,234 | 3,472 |
| Change in man's earnings ($) | 2,697 | 3,260 | 3,303 | 3,248 | 5,252 |
| Change in woman's relative income | 0.052 | 0.122 | 0.156 | 0.067 | 0.092 |
| Change in woman's occupational prestige | 523 | −397 | −557 | −229 | −617 |
| Change in man's occupational prestige | 710 | −1,003 | 668 | −374 | −772 |
| Change in woman's relative occupational prestige | −0.146 | 0.146 | −0.719 | −0.107 | −0.114 |

**Figure 8.3:** Multivariate modeling strategy for predicting Wave 2 housework class

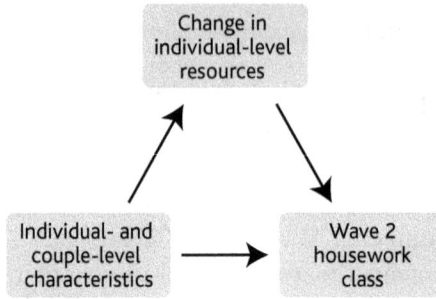

**Table 8.6:** Results of multivariate models predicting Wave 2 housework class membership

| Resource | Effect of resource statistically significant? |
|---|---|
| Change in woman's average weekly work hours | Yes |
| Change in man's average weekly work hours | No |
| Change in woman's earnings ($) | Yes |
| Change in man's earnings ($) | No |
| Change in woman's relative income (%) | Yes |
| Change in woman's occupational prestige | Yes |
| Change in man's occupational prestige | Yes |
| Change in woman's relative occupational prestige (%) | Yes |

greatest among men who were in the Traditional class, being a little over three hours. Consistent with the findings in Table 8.3, there is evidence of gender-deviance neutralization among Traditional couples. Couples where men had the greatest reduction of work hours and women had the greatest increase in income were most likely to be in the Traditional class in Wave 2. We see evidence of men's power over time in securing their place as breadwinners in women's reduction of hours for couples who were in the Ultra-Traditional class at the second interview. As would be expected, couples whose work hours and occupational prestige remained stable over the two interviews but who earned more income were most likely to be in the Egalitarian High Workload class. We see evidence of the time availability perspective as well as women's ability to exert power in their relationship in couples who were in the Egalitarian class in Wave 2. The men in those couples had the second-greatest decline in work hours despite earning more money; the men seemed to be using their time to perform more housework.

The couples in the Transitional Husbands class are those where men do more housework than men in the Traditional class but less than men in the Egalitarian class. Across the two interviews, couples who were in the Transitional Husbands class in Wave 2 were comprised of men who worked fewer hours and women who had the greatest reduction in relative occupational prestige (though because women's relative occupational prestige was above 1 at the first interview, as noted in Table 5.3, the small absolute changes seem larger than they are). We find evidence of the challenge of being men across the two time periods reflected in the Transitional Husbands class. These men are performing more housework than are men in the two more traditional classes while attempting to navigate their place as men in the paid labor market. Further, their wives are navigating their position in the labor market as well. We find evidence of women's latent power in the Transitional Husbands class as these were couples who saw an absolute increase in men's income and relative occupational prestige but also saw women's relative income rise. The combination of those changes in the relationship with the labor market as a couple is reflected in men being likely to perform more housework than would be expected (but not at the same level as their wives). Women were able to secure more housework from men as men worked fewer paid labor hours and women contributed greater earnings to the home. Overall, these descriptive results are consistent with the multivariate findings reported in Table 8.6 as only the change in the man's work hours and earnings are not significant predictors of Wave 2 class once other characteristics are included in the analysis.

## Summary

One possible measure of latent power is the extent to which one can secure change in others' behavior. This chapter presents evidence of couples changing their individual-level behaviors in response to the power dynamics that led to their division of housework. For couples in all classes except the Ultra-Traditional class, the housework dynamic at Time 1 led to changes in both women's and men's occupational choice that were consistent with the reduction in cognitive dissonance among the individuals (and couples as a unit). Couples worked to get their working lives to be more consistent with their division of housework responsibilities. This is despite, or maybe in addition to, the connection between labor-market characteristics and housework class membership in Wave 1 documented in Chapter 5. However, the couples in the Ultra-Traditional class in Wave 1 showed striking consistency from

Wave 1 to Wave 2 in the spouses' relationships with the labor market, suggesting the strength of the underlying ideological underpinnings of the behaviors of those in the Ultra-Traditional class.

Our data did not provide the robust evidence that we expected as we sought to connect resources and the utilization of latent, hidden, and/ or overt power through the examination of housework over the family life course (at least in the five years between Wave 1 and Wave 2 of the NSFH). However, we were able to document ways in which both women and men were able to alter their partners' behavior across the housework classes. As we have noted before, the connection between housework class and power dynamics is not deterministic. The path of least resistance, including maintaining the status quo, is a powerful social process in and of itself regardless of the possible ways in which individuals could potentially exert power to exact change.

While maintaining class membership reflects consistency within couples in their joint relationships to the public and private spheres, changes in resources and the relationship with the labor market differentially impacted couples in ways that did reveal evidence of both women's and men's ability to change their partners' behavior. Couples where women secured more economic resources at a pace similar to their husbands were more likely to be more egalitarian; women securing resources while men did not was likely to lead to gender-deviance neutralization and a traditional division of labor at the second interview. Women's ability to use power secured from the public sphere to create more equal conditions in the private sphere was hampered by men's own connections to the labor market. The cultural norms that continue to subtly suggest that men must be primary earners even if not breadwinners in order to be considered masculine also continue to undermine women's ability to secure an equal partner in household responsibilities.

Another way in which couples exert power is through the intergenerational transmission of norms. Chapter 9 examines the housework time of the adult children of the couples in our five housework classes to document the extent to which power dynamics in the family of origin transmit to adult households.

# 9

# Housework and socialization

## Introduction

Power dynamics in one's family of origin shape internalized notions of normative family relationships. Previous research has documented how the division of paid and unpaid work in one's family of origin socializes children to hold specific attitudes and beliefs about how relationships should work, as well as provides a model for how to divide paid and unpaid tasks (for example, Cunningham, 2001; Gupta, 2006; Álvarez and Miles-Touya, 2012). In this chapter, we examine the extent to which the housework class membership of one's parents shapes the performance of housework tasks of adult children once they have an independent household. The adult children of the couples in the National Survey of Families and Households (NSFH) were interviewed in 2001/02. They provided information about their own housework performance. While we do not have data from the adult children's partners reporting their own housework time or attitudes about the gendered division of labor, we do have information about partners' labor-market participation, absolute and relative resources, and demographic characteristics as reported by the adult child during the interview. Using the adult children's reports, we can document the extent to which children's personal performance of housework may have been informed by their parents', especially regarding the internalization of gendered task performance. Housework performance is a dynamic process that is a reflection of negotiation not only with one's partner, but also with one's past as it informs the overall work patterns considered to be appropriate for adult women and men.

We perform latent profile analysis (LPA) on the adult children of the couples in our analytic sample from the NSFH. These data were collected approximately 14 years after the first NSFH wave, allowing for a sufficient amount of time for the children to have left their parents' home and establish an independent household. We have data from only the adult children, not their partners, so we are unable to perform the couple-based LPA that we did for the children's parents. Instead, we present the patterns of housework task performance among the female and male children separately, noting that part of the division of housework that led to the construction of the five classes among the NSFH couples (the parents of these adult children) was a distribution of tasks by the gender of the partner. The first section of the chapter documents the class demonstrated among the adult children, noting gender differences in task performance. After describing the adult children's housework classes, we compare the class memberships using many of the key characteristics that we used to describe their parents' housework classes in Chapter 5. We then present an analysis of the possible intergenerational transmission of housework labor task performance by focusing our attention on parental housework class. We conclude the chapter with an examination of the housework class consequences for these adult children in a manner similar to that which we performed for their parents in Chapter 6.

## Constructing the child housework classes

Using data from the third wave of the NSFH (see Sweet et al, 1988), we used LPA to classify 447 adult children who were married (260 women and 187 men) into gender-specific classes (for methodological details on the gender-specific LPA, see Tables A7 and A8 in the Appendix). This analysis yielded three distinct classes among both women and men. As we have data from the children of the NSFH participants but not their spouses, we are unable to directly replicate the analyses in Chapters 4 and 5. As was the case with their parents, the housework classes among the adult children were determined by examining the average amount of time that the individual spent on nine housework tasks: meal preparation, kitchen work, cleaning, grocery shopping, doing laundry, paying bills, performing yardwork, performing car maintenance, and driving for the household. The patterns that emerged from the LPA reflect three classes that demonstrate differences in the tasks that the women and men perform as individuals in married couples.

## Women's housework classes

We labeled the three housework classes demonstrated by the adult female children as "Ultra-Traditional," "Traditional," and "Nontraditional" based upon how they divided their time across the nine household tasks. Figure 9.1 displays the overall patterns of the division of housework tasks by all three classes simultaneously. As with their parents, we also categorized housework as traditionally feminine tasks, neutral tasks, and traditionally masculine tasks. The data are taken from Table A9 in the Appendix. The adult female children

**Figure 9.1:** Housework distribution across all classes: female children

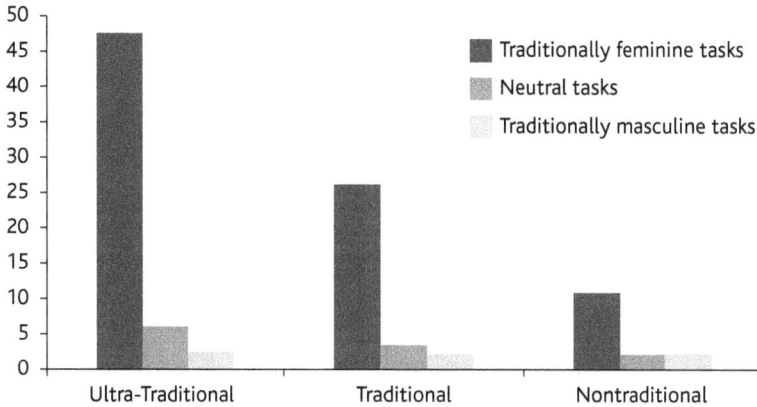

performed very few hours of the traditionally masculine tasks regardless of their housework class category. Therefore, the class categorization was derived from the distinctions in the performance of traditionally feminine and neutral tasks. Women in the Ultra-Traditional class spent significantly more time on traditionally feminine tasks than did women in the Traditional or Nontraditional classes, while also reporting spending more time on neutral tasks as well. Women in the Traditional class reported overall housework time consistent with the women (the mothers) in the Traditional class in our sample. The Nontraditional women performed the least amount of housework overall among the adult female children.

Figure 9.2 documents the distribution of tasks among the adult female children who were categorized as part of the Ultra-Traditional class. These women reported spending over 18 hours per week on cleaning, approximately eight hours on laundry and kitchen work, and almost ten hours on meal preparation. Compared to the mothers categorized as the most traditional (those in the Ultra-Traditional class), the Ultra-Traditional adult female children performed less overall housework (see Figure 4.3). Specifically, the younger women spent fewer hours on meal preparation and kitchen tasks, as well as on yardwork. Slightly more time is spent by younger women on driving than among the older Ultra-Traditional women.

Figure 9.3 documents the distribution of tasks among the adult female children who were categorized as part of the Traditional class. These women spent approximately six hours a week each on meal preparation, kitchen work, and cleaning, distinguishing them from women in the Ultra-Traditional class. These adult female children

**Figure 9.2:** Ultra-Traditional female children's housework task distribution

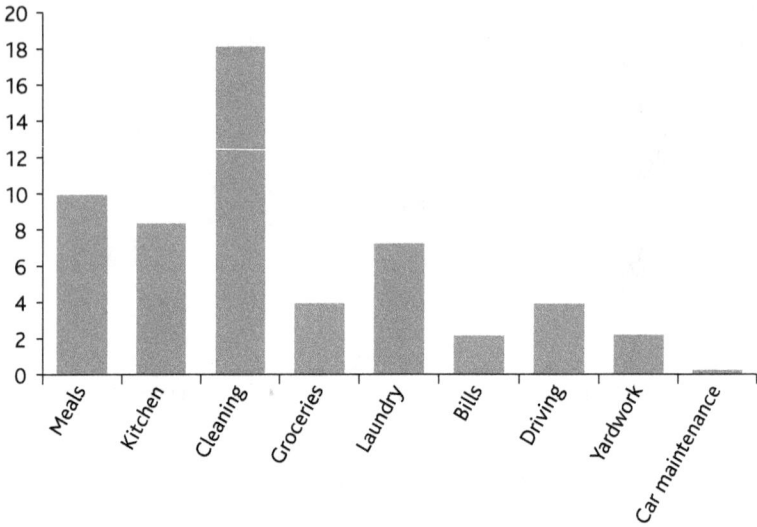

**Figure 9.3:** Traditional female children's housework task distribution

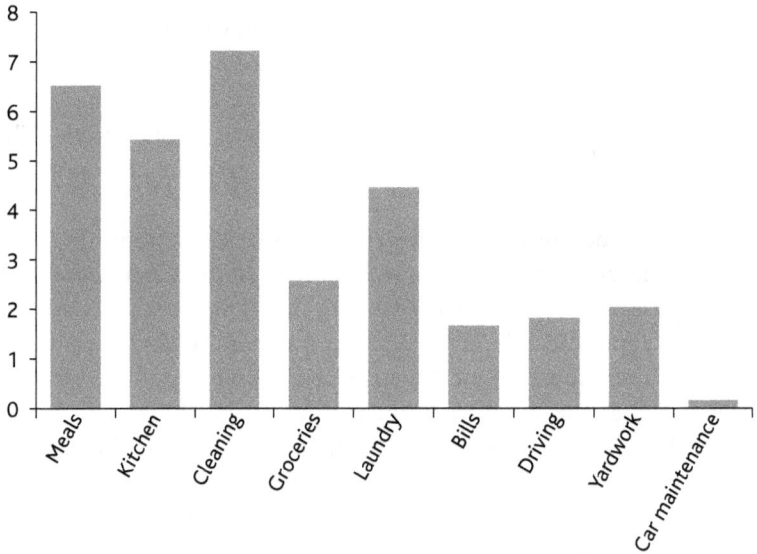

performed tasks in a manner similar to the second most traditionally gendered class among their parents, the Traditional class (see Figure 4.5). Notably, the younger women spent a little more time on cleaning and laundry, as well as yardwork, as compared to the older women in the Traditional class.

Figure 9.4 documents the distribution of tasks among the adult female children who were categorized as Nontraditional. As noted earlier, women in the Nontraditional class performed less housework overall. The pattern of time spent on housework tasks among women in the Nontraditional class is similar to that of women in the Traditional class, with one exception: the distribution of time spent on neutral tasks. Women in the Nontraditional class spent approximately the same amount of time on paying bills and driving, whereas women in the Traditional class spent twice as much time driving as on paying bills. In comparison to the women in couples categorized as not traditional (the women in the Egalitarian couples, see Figure 4.9), these adult female children spent substantially less time on all feminine tasks.

**Figure 9.4:** Nontraditional female children's housework task distribution

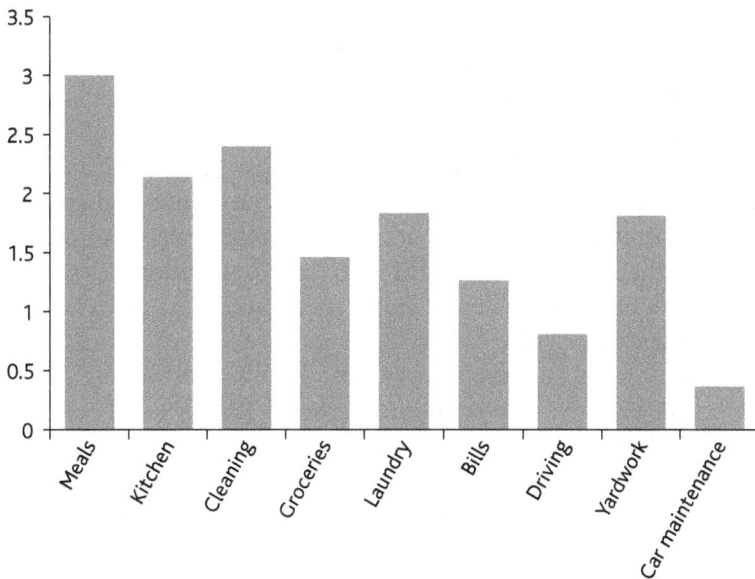

## Men's housework classes

Based on the distribution of tasks, we labeled the three housework classes documented among the adult male children as "Traditional," "Transitional," and "Nontraditional." Figure 9.5 displays the overall patterns of male housework performance as well as the distribution of tasks over the traditionally feminine, neutral, and masculine tasks; the data are taken from Table A10 in the Appendix. Men in the Traditional class performed the least amount of housework overall, though like the

**Figure 9.5:** Housework distribution across all classes: male children

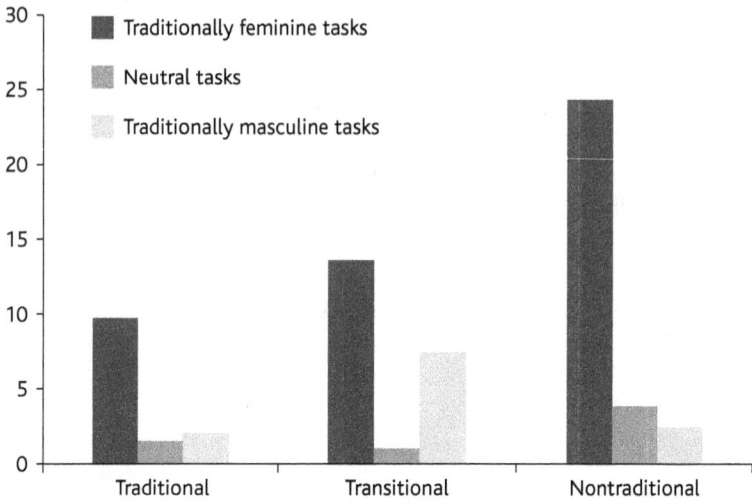

men in the Transitional and Nontraditional classes, they spent more time on traditionally feminine tasks than on neutral or traditionally masculine tasks. Men in the Transitional class spent more time on traditionally feminine tasks than did men in the Traditional class but also performed more traditionally masculine tasks than did men in either of the other two classes. Men in the Nontraditional class spent more time on traditionally feminine and neutral tasks than did men in the other two classes.

Figure 9.6 displays the housework task distribution among the adult male children who were categorized as Traditional. These men performed relatively little housework compared to other men. Among the traditionally feminine tasks, they spent the most time on meal preparation, a task for which there has been substantial branding of the work as masculine during the time that these men came of age (including the rise of cooking shows with men as head chefs and the popularization of outdoor and indoor grilling). These adult male children's housework time distribution most closely resembles the housework time of men in the Transitional Husbands class among their parents (see Figure 4.7).

Figure 9.7 displays the housework task distribution among the adult male children who were categorized as Transitional. Given the similarities in task time for individual feminine (specifically meal preparation, kitchen work, and cleaning) and masculine tasks, the men in the Transitional class are demonstrating behavior consistent with gender–deviance neutralization (Greenstein, 2000). They overperform

**Figure 9.6:** Traditional male children's housework task distribution

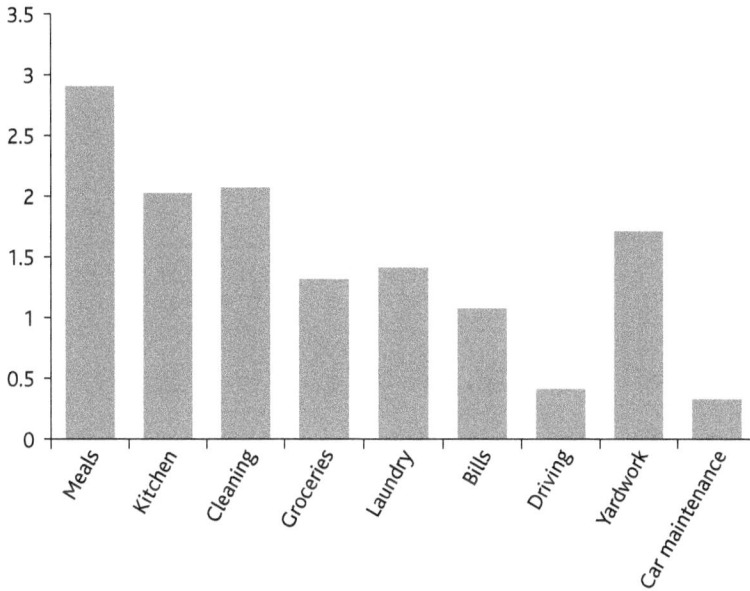

**Figure 9.7:** Transitional male children's housework task distribution

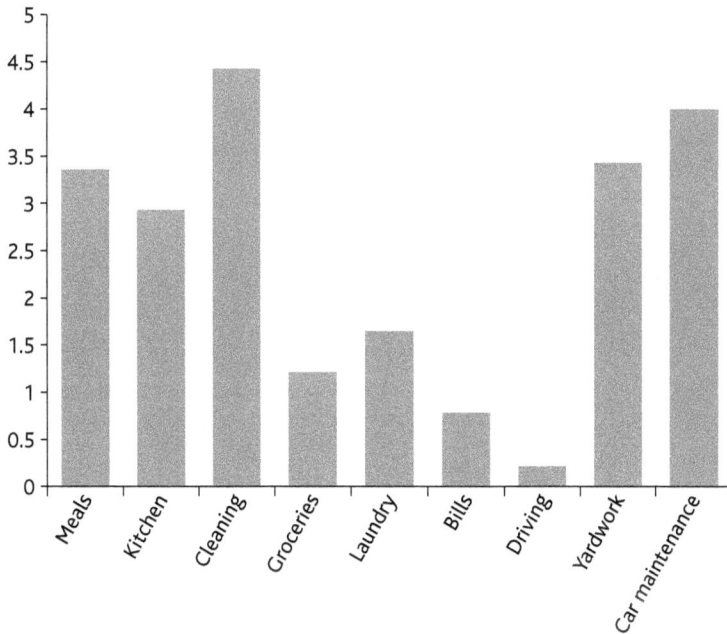

on masculine tasks to compensate for their time on feminine tasks. Among the older men—the fathers in the NSFH sample—there is no class of couples where men display a similar distribution of housework time.

Figure 9.8 displays the housework task distribution among the adult male children who were categorized as part of the Nontraditional class. The distribution of housework time for men in the Nontraditional class mirrors that of adult female children in the Traditional class. These individuals spent substantial time on meal preparation, kitchen work, and cleaning, with laundry garnering slightly less time. They spent less time overall on groceries, paying bills, and driving, and little time on traditionally masculine tasks overall. The adult male children categorized as Nontraditional had a distribution of housework task time most similar to men in the parental Egalitarian housework class. The key differences were that younger men performed more cleaning and less yardwork than their most similar older counterparts.

**Figure 9.8:** Nontraditional male children's housework task distribution

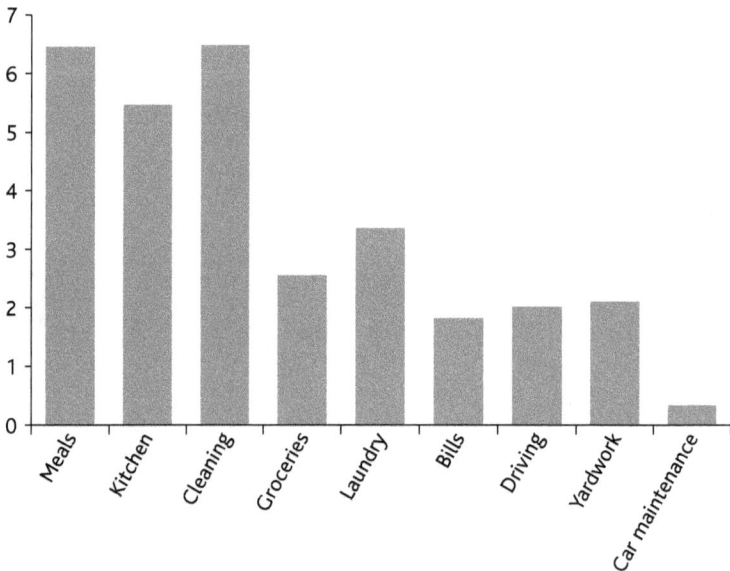

## Adult children's housework class characteristics

In Chapter 5, we presented the key characteristics of the five classes in order to describe the couples who comprise them. In the next section of this chapter, we describe each of the three classes that emerged from the LPA of the adult children of our NSFH analytic sample. We begin here as we did in Chapter 5 by initially focusing on measures of the theoretical frameworks explaining the time spent on housework tasks (for more details of the measures used to describe the classes, see the Appendix).

As we can see from Table 9.1, there are modest but statistically significant differences in work hours reported for women and men by the adult children in the sample. The work hours reported by female adult children for themselves and their spouses across classes mirror the pattern documented among the women's parents (see Table 5.1). There is a substantial gap among the spouses in the most traditional housework class that narrows as women's distribution of housework becomes less traditional. The average weekly work hours reported by the male adult children for themselves also follow the pattern documented among their parents, with men reporting fewer work hours as the distribution of housework becomes less traditional. However, the paid work hours that the adult male children report for their wives do not match the pattern documented for their mothers relative to housework performance. Interestingly, these men's reports of their wives' work hours are not statistically significantly different from one another. Overall, the typical pattern of men's less traditional housework task time and distribution being more likely to occur among men working fewer hours for pay per week holds among the adult children of the NSFH sample whether reported by the adult daughters or sons.

Women in the Ultra-Traditional class are statistically significantly distinct (as are their husbands) from the other classes in that the women earn less and have lower educational attainment, as shown in Table 9.2. Their husbands earn less than do men married to women in the Traditional class. Women in the Traditional class are very similar to their husbands in both earnings and educational attainment. The women in the Nontraditional class report earning significantly more

**Table 9.1:** Adult child class membership and average labor-market hours per week

|  | Female adult children | | | Male adult children | | |
|---|---|---|---|---|---|---|
|  | Ultra-Traditional | Trad-itional | Non-traditional | Trad-itional | Transi-tional | Non-traditional |
| Woman's average weekly work hours | 31.6 | 39.4 | 40.5 | 40.8 | 34.0 | 41.8 |
| Man's average weekly work hours | 46.3 | 43.3 | 40.5 | 41.6 | 41.5 | 31.3 |

**Table 9.2:** Adult child class membership and absolute resources

| | Female adult children | | | Male adult children | | |
|---|---|---|---|---|---|---|
| | Ultra-Traditional | Trad-itional | Non-traditional | Trad-itional | Transi-tional | Non-traditional |
| Woman's earnings ($) | 10,004 | 26,679 | 27,848 | 19,493 | 9,750 | 31,010 |
| Man's earnings ($) | 20,240 | 29,244 | 18,805 | 29,111 | 25,834 | 14,348 |
| Woman's educational attainment | 12.3 | 13.3 | 13.5 | 13.7 | 14.7 | 13.3 |
| Man's educational attainment | 11.3 | 13.6 | 13.6 | 13.7 | 12.2 | 13.1 |

than do their husbands. This pattern is not only consistent with bargaining theory, but is also consistent with the relationship that these women had seen in their parents' homes, where women with fewer resources performed more housework overall and more traditionally feminine tasks (compare with Table 5.2).

Bargaining theory is also evidenced in the relationship between the adult male children's reports of their (and their wives') earnings and educational attainment and the men's class membership. There is also evidence of an intergenerational transmission of behaviors among the male children as the patterns of reported income for the men in the Traditional and Transitional classes mirror those of their fathers in the Transitional and Egalitarian classes (see Table 5.2). Without reports of the wives' housework time, we cannot match the classes intergenerationally (as we note later in this chapter), but the pattern is suggestive. What is most interesting is that the adult male children in the Nontraditional housework class report earning substantially less money than do their wives. None of the housework classes in the NSFH sample were characterized by women out-earning men. However, that the men in the Nontraditional class do report being out-earned by their wives is additional evidence for bargaining theory, and, in addition, evidence of women's increased ability to leverage resources as power in their households. The data on women's relative education and income in Table 9.3 also provide support for bargaining theory beyond what was evidenced among the parents (see Table 5.3). Women report performing less housework and less traditionally feminine housework when they have greater relative economic resources; men report performing more housework (including traditionally feminine tasks) when their wives have greater relative economic resources.

**Table 9.3:** Adult child class membership and relative resources

| | Female adult children | | | Male adult children | | |
|---|---|---|---|---|---|---|
| | Ultra-Traditional | Trad-itional | Non-traditional | Trad-itional | Transi-tional | Non-traditional |
| Woman's relative education | 1.505 | 1.301 | 1.012 | 0.996 | 1.207 | 1.005 |
| Women's relative income | 0.657 | 0.578 | 0.542 | 0.669 | 0.377 | 2.161 |

Table 9.4 presents overall demographic characteristics for the adult children of the NSFH sample based upon their determined housework class. Demographically, the women whose housework class membership is more traditional have also been married statistically significantly longer and have statistically significantly more children under the age of five than do women who are members of a less traditional housework class. While men who are in the Traditional or Transitional class are statistically similar to one another in their marital duration and number of children, Nontraditional men are significantly different, having been married longer and having more children under the age of five.

**Table 9.4:** Adult child class membership and demographic characteristics

| | Female adult children | | | Male adult children | | |
|---|---|---|---|---|---|---|
| | Ultra-Traditional | Trad-itional | Non-traditional | Trad-itional | Transi-tional | Non-traditional |
| **Couple characteristics** | | | | | | |
| Marital duration | 7.470 | 5.670 | 5.091 | 4.518 | 4.854 | 5.772 |
| Number of children (under age 5) | 1.000 | 0.730 | 0.267 | 0.441 | 0.462 | 0.804 |
| **Individual characteristics** | | | | | | |
| Respondent gender ideology | 13.353 | 13.112 | 13.149 | 13.325 | 14.286 | 12.655 |
| White | 0.875 | 1.000 | 0.927 | 0.948 | 1.000 | 0.867 |
| Black | 0.125 | 0 | 0.024 | 0 | 0 | 0.100 |
| Hispanic | 0 | 0 | 0.049 | 0.034 | 0 | 0.033 |
| Other race | 0 | 0 | 0 | 0.017 | 0 | 0 |
| **Religion** | | | | | | |
| Protestant | 0.457 | 0.433 | 0.314 | 0.287 | 0.429 | 0.321 |
| Catholic | 0 | 0.016 | 0.022 | 0.008 | 0 | 0 |
| Other religion | 0.171 | 0.189 | 0.197 | 0.223 | 0.286 | 0.196 |
| No religion | 0.371 | 0.362 | 0.467 | 0.481 | 0.286 | 0.482 |

## Intergenerational transmission of the gendered division of housework

As with other social roles, research has investigated the extent to which the division of paid and unpaid labor is transmitted from one generation to the next (Cunningham, 2001; Gupta, 2006). Here, we document the distribution of adult child housework class membership across parental housework classes. Table 9.5 demonstrates the distribution of adult child class membership across the five classes by which the parents were categorized. There is some evidence of the intergenerational transmission of housework in this sample as female adult children who were classified as Ultra–Traditional did not have parents who were classified as Egalitarian or Egalitarian High Workload. Adult female children who were categorized as either Traditional or Nontraditional had parents who were classified in very similar ways at the first NSFH interview. There were no differences or specific patterns among adult male children's housework class membership and their parents' class membership.

Table 9.6 examines parental housework class stability/change over time and adult child housework class membership. As a reminder, the adult children were themselves interviewed a decade after Wave 2. The experience of stability/change over time between Waves 1 and 2 was occurring just prior to when the adult children were themselves marrying and establishing their joint households. Therefore, watching parents navigate and potentially modify their division of housework from an adult point of view may be particularly salient for the performance of housework among the adult children.

That the majority of parents experienced some sort of egalitarian shift in the division of housework between Waves 1 and 2 is reflected

**Table 9.5:** Parent and adult child housework class distribution

| Parental housework class membership (%) | Female adult children | | | Male adult children | | |
|---|---|---|---|---|---|---|
| | Ultra-Traditional | Trad-itional | Non-traditional | Trad-itional | Transi-tional | Non-traditional |
| Ultra-Traditional | 12.5 | 23.1 | 12.2 | 20.0 | 50.0 | 26.7 |
| Traditional | 75.0 | 50.0 | 62.2 | 53.0 | 37.5 | 50.0 |
| Transitional Husbands | 12.5 | 11.5 | 9.7 | 8.3 | 12.5 | 6.7 |
| Egalitarian | 0 | 7.7 | 8.5 | 10.0 | 0 | 10.0 |
| Egalitarian High Workload | 0 | 7.7 | 7.3 | 8.3 | 0 | 6.7 |

in the majority of the adult children, regardless of their own housework time, having been raised in a household that became more egalitarian. Adult female children raised in households where parents became more egalitarian in their housework across the two waves were less likely to be part of the Ultra-Traditional class than to be in the Traditional or Nontraditional classes. Experiencing a shift in the division of labor toward a more egalitarian split of housework provided insight into a greater variety of options for how women could contribute to housework time, reducing the strict attachment to performing all of the housework tasks as the only approach. Stagnancy in parental housework class over time yielded a greater likelihood for adult women to be in the Ultra-Traditional class. It is likely that not having experienced their parents actively negotiating the division of housework discouraged women from negotiating their own housework time, opting instead to accept the path of least resistance and perform substantial amounts of housework in their own homes. The transition in parental housework class that is reflected among most parents across Wave 1 to Wave 2 was likely the result of discussion, negotiation, and debate between parents. As noted in Chapter 6, women in the Traditional class were least likely to report disagreements over housework, while women in all other classes were equally as likely to report disagreements. Female children growing up in a household where there was little disagreement around housework performance and little change in the distribution of the work over time may have internalized that the appropriate way to perform gender in a married relationship is to perform the majority of the housework. Indeed, the adult female children categorized as Ultra-Traditional report housework hours similar to those found among women in the parental housework class of Traditional. Thus, the amount of discussion, negotiation, and debate between the parents of these female

**Table 9.6:** Parental housework class stability and adult child class membership

| Parental housework class membership transition (%) | Female adult children | | | Male adult children | | |
|---|---|---|---|---|---|---|
| | Ultra-Traditional | Trad-itional | Non-traditional | Trad-itional | Transit-ional | Non-traditional |
| Became more traditional | 12.5 | 19.2 | 18.3 | 16.7 | 0 | 20.0 |
| Became more egalitarian | 50.0 | 61.5 | 58.5 | 60.0 | 50.0 | 50.0 |
| Stayed the same | 37.5 | 19.2 | 23.1 | 23.3 | 50.0 | 30.0 |

adult children seems to have reinforced gendered behavior as measured by the women's housework performance.

The intergenerational transmission of housework time is more complicated for men, in some ways reflecting the challenges of contemporary manhood as constructed in heterosexual relationships. Men who experienced a traditional shift in the parental division of labor were almost equally likely to be in the Traditional or Nontraditional classes. Taken together with the increased likelihood of men who experienced an egalitarian shift in the parental division of labor being in the Traditional class, these findings suggest that the cultural path of least resistance for men to perform little housework is quite strong. Men whose parents negotiated a more egalitarian division of labor were differentially likely to have had parents report of disagreements about housework. Wilcox and Nock (2006) found that couples with egalitarian spouses reported lower marital quality, in part, because of the constant negotiation of what was considered fair and equitable; those negotiations were not needed in traditional couples as the cultural scripts for their behavior were readily at hand. Men, for whom a traditional division of labor has benefits as they perform little of the work, were more comfortable following the cultural scripts when they had experienced conflict around constructing a more egalitarian division of labor in their childhood home. That men whose parents' housework class was stable over time were more likely to be in the Transitional or Nontraditional class also supports this interpretation.

## Predicting adult child housework class membership

The previous analyses have examined differences in class membership one characteristic at a time. As with the parents' analysis in Chapter 5, we also present the results of the best fitting statistical model that includes multiple characteristics simultaneously. As with the parents of these adult children, we employ multinomial logistic regression using Traditional class membership as the reference category for both the female and male adult children. To be consistent with our earlier findings on the parents presented in Chapter 5, we present the odds ratios resulting from our analysis. As a reminder, odds ratios are interpreted as the odds that an individual will be classified as the specific class (for example, Ultra-Traditional) versus being classified as Traditional given a change in a particular predictor (for example, an increase in the woman's income), net of the effects of all of the other characteristics included in the model. That is, if the odds ratio is greater than 1, an increase in the predictor increases the likelihood of being in the specific class relative to the Traditional class; if the odds ratio is less than 1, an increase in the predictor decreases the likelihood of being in the specific class relative to the Traditional class. As the best fitting models differ by the gender of the adult child, Table 9.7 presents the results for the female adult children and Table 9.8 presents the results for the male adult children.

The best fitting statistical model predicting female adult child class membership has only two predictors: the hours that the husband is reported to spend in the labor market and the number of children under the age of five. Women are less likely to be categorized as Nontraditional (relative to Traditional) the more hours that their husband works and the more children under the age of five that they have. In subsequent analyses, we examined whether there was a direct intergenerational transmission of housework class membership net of other characteristics; there was no statistical relationship between parental class membership and adult female child class membership net of other adult female child characteristics.

The best fitting statistical model predicting male adult child class membership includes measures of time availability, absolute resources,

**Table 9.7**: Predicting female adult child class membership

| Characteristic | Ultra-Traditional (versus Traditional) | Nontraditional (versus Traditional) |
|---|---|---|
| **Time availability** | | |
| Man's average weekly work hours | 1.036 | 0.971* |
| **Other** | | |
| Number of children under the age of 5 | 1.222 | 0.349* |

Note: *$p < .05$.

**Table 9.8**: Predicting male adult child class membership

| Characteristic | Transitional (versus Traditional) | Nontraditional (versus Traditional) |
|---|---|---|
| **Time availability** | | |
| Man's average weekly work hours | 1.039 | 0.941* |
| **Absolute resources** | | |
| Woman's income | 0.999 | 1.001* |
| Man's income | 0.999 | 0.999* |
| Man's educational attainment | 0.615* | 0.712* |
| **Couple characteristics** | | |
| Number of children under the age of 5 | 2.475* | 1.591* |
| Marital duration | 0.998 | 1.175* |

Note: *$p < .10$.

and couple characteristics. Men who report working more hours are statistically significantly less likely to be members of the Nontraditional class relative to the Traditional class, as are men with more education and higher incomes. Consistent with the descriptive analysis, men married for longer and with more children are more likely to be in the Nontraditional class than in the Traditional class. Men with more education are significantly less likely to be in the Transitional class than the Traditional class but more likely when they have more children under the age of five.

As with the adult female children, we performed subsequent analyses examining whether there was a direct intergenerational transmission of housework class membership net of other characteristics; as with the adult female children, there was no statistical relationship between parental class membership and adult male child class membership net of other adult male child characteristics. Overall, while there may not be statistical evidence for an intergenerational transmission of housework class membership, there is one pattern in behavior that can be documented: the more time that men spend in paid work, the more likely their housework time is lower and not spent on traditionally feminine tasks. Table 5.8 documents this pattern for the fathers and Table 9.8 documents this pattern for sons. More than anything, these two findings demonstrate the continued power of the labor market over men's time, solidifying over two generations the connection between paid labor, rather than reproductive labor, and men's time.

## Adult child housework class consequences

As we argued in Chapter 5, latent and hidden power could potentially be evidenced by examining the extent to which one's spouse is working the number of hours in the labor market that one prefers. Chapter 6 demonstrated that there was evidence of the use of latent and hidden power among men in the Ultra-Traditional and Traditional couples. In this section, we first examine whether there may be evidence of the exercise of latent and hidden power among the adult children of the couples in our NSFH sample. We then examine where there may be an intergenerational transmission of the exercise of latent and hidden power.

### Preferred labor-market participation

Table 9.9 demonstrates that all of the adult children wish to be working fewer hours in the labor market and wish that their spouses

**Table 9.9:** Adult child class membership and preferred labor-market hours

| | Female adult children | | | Male adult children | | |
|---|---|---|---|---|---|---|
| | Ultra-Traditional | Trad-itional | Non-traditional | Trad-itional | Transi-tional | Non-traditional |
| Actual working hours | 31.6 | 39.4 | 40.5 | 41.6 | 41.4 | 31.3 |
| Preferred working hours for self | 29.2 | 27.7 | 32.9 | 32.7 | 42.0 | 27.6 |
| Difference between preferred and actual working hours for self | −2.4 | −11.6 | −7.6 | −8.9 | 0.6 | −3.7 |
| Spouse actual working hours | 46.3 | 43.2 | 40.5 | 40.8 | 34.0 | 41.8 |
| Preferred working hours for spouse | 38.9 | 33.6 | 27.6 | 27.7 | 34.4 | 35.1 |
| Difference between preferred and actual working hours for spouse | −7.4 | −9.6 | −12.9 | −13.1 | 0.4 | −6.7 |

were working fewer hours as well. The one exception is Transitional men as they report that both they and their spouses are quite close to the respondent's desired labor-market participation levels. If latent power was being exercised, we would expect to see that men in the Traditional class would report small differences between their wives' actual and preferred work hours; however, quite the opposite, this is the group that reports the greatest difference between actual and preferred labor-market hours. Perhaps men in the Traditional class (who report a traditionally gendered performance of housework) believe that their wives' working hours are interfering with the performance of household responsibilities. They are not the most traditional in their gender ideology (see Table 9.4), but they could be attempting to articulate what they believe the gendered division of paid and unpaid work should be through their response to the question about preferred work hours for their spouses. This could be indicative of a desire to shape their spouses' behavior, that is, to use latent or hidden power, which has not yet come to fruition.

The same logic can be applied to Nontraditional women's responses regarding preferred working hours for their spouses. Through their responses, they report preferring that both they and their spouses (who work approximately the same number of hours) work fewer hours, with a greater reduction preferred for their spouses. This report could be indicative of these women wanting to exert latent or hidden power in their relationship in order for their husbands to be more available to perform the housework tasks that the Nontraditional women themselves are not performing. Overall, however, we do not see clear evidence of the use of latent/hidden power among the adult children of our NSFH sample around the issue of preferred labor-market hours.

In Table 9.10 and Table 9.11, we situate adult female and male child preferred labor-market hours at the intersection of their own and their parents' housework classes. In these tables, we attempt to identify whether there are patterns in the influence of how the performance of housework shapes preferred labor-market hours. Remember that Ultra-Traditional fathers seemed to desire a very gendered division of labor and couples in the Transitional Husbands and Egalitarian High Workload classes seemed to want behavioral consistency (see Chapter 6). Here, we do see some indication that parental housework class shapes how adult children use their own housework performance as a lens to describe their own desired relationship dynamics. Keep in mind the very small sample sizes within each of the groups, thereby affording us only a brief glance into the possible patterns. For example, Nontraditional women whose parents were Egalitarian High Workload report their preferred work hours for themselves and their spouses as quite close to their actual work hours. This may be the result of Nontraditional women whose parents were Egalitarian High Workload seeing the importance of selecting a spouse who is as committed to egalitarianism as they are. Latent power in its definitional form, where disputes do not happen because of past resolution in one's favor, could be the mechanism through which these work behaviors have developed.

Traditional men whose parents were either Ultra-Traditional or Traditional report a strong desire for their wives to be more present at home and spend less time in the labor market. As discussed earlier, these men may be signaling a desire to exert power in their relationships but have not yet been able to do so. Interestingly, Traditional men whose parents were either in the Transitional Husbands or Egalitarian High Workload classes report the lowest preferred work hours for themselves and their spouses across all of the adult male children. These men may be seeking a way to mimic the unique balance that their parents had around the performance of housework by seeking ways for them and their spouses to both be available to do more at home.

Overall, the Nontraditional men seem to want to find ways to support their housework performance with a focus on wanting to make changes (in general) to their own labor-market time.

Table 9.10: Parental housework class membership, female adult child class membership, and preferred labor-market hours

| | Ultra-Traditional | Traditional | Transitional Husband | Egalitarian | Egalitarian High Workload |
|---|---|---|---|---|---|
| **Ultra-Traditional** | | | | | |
| Actual working hours | 0 | 33.3 | 10.0 | — | — |
| Preferred working hours for self | 8.0 | 23.2 | 10.0 | — | — |
| Difference between preferred and actual working hours for self | 8.0 | –10.1 | 0 | — | — |
| Spouse actual working hours | 50.0 | 40.0 | 40.0 | — | — |
| Preferred working hours for spouse | 40.0 | 40.0 | 20.0 | — | — |
| Difference between preferred and actual working hours for spouse | –10.0 | 0 | –20.0 | — | — |
| **Traditional** | | | | | |
| Actual working hours | 51.6 | 39.3 | 37.5 | 41.5 | 40.0 |
| Preferred working hours for self | 21.5 | 27.4 | 28.3 | 34.5 | 25.0 |
| Difference between preferred and actual working hours for self | –30.1 | –11.9 | –9.2 | –7.0 | –15.0 |
| Spouse actual working hours | 42.2 | 45.0 | 31.7 | 29.5 | 40.0 |
| Preferred working hours for spouse | 32.0 | 37.5 | 21.7 | 40.0 | 10.0 |
| Difference between preferred and actual working hours for spouse | –12.2 | –7.5 | –10.0 | 10.5 | –30.0 |
| **Nontraditional** | | | | | |
| Actual working hours | 35.0 | 39.1 | 44.5 | 48.0 | 34.0 |
| Preferred working hours for self | 30.7 | 35.8 | 24.9 | 38.6 | 33.5 |
| Difference between preferred and actual working hours for self | –4.3 | –3.3 | –19.6 | –9.4 | –0.5 |
| Spouse actual working hours | 44.3 | 43.4 | 37.9 | 36.0 | 33.6 |
| Preferred working hours for spouse | 32.9 | 26.9 | 21.8 | 31.0 | 27.2 |
| Difference between preferred and actual working hours for spouse | –11.4 | –16.5 | –16.1 | –5.0 | –6.4 |

Table **9.11**: Parental housework class membership, male adult child class membership, and preferred labor-market hours

| | Ultra-Traditional | Traditional | Transitional Husband | Egalitarian | Egalitarian High Workload |
|---|---|---|---|---|---|
| **Traditional** | | | | | |
| Actual working hours | 45.1 | 41.0 | 31.8 | 47.5 | 45.0 |
| Preferred working hours for self | 36.1 | 34.5 | 19.8 | 35.7 | 27.4 |
| Difference between preferred and actual working hours for self | −9.0 | −6.5 | −12.0 | −11.8 | −17.6 |
| Spouse actual working hours | 40.0 | 44.7 | 25.0 | 33.8 | 45.0 |
| Preferred working hours for spouse | 27.1 | 29.7 | 19.8 | 27.3 | 15.0 |
| Difference between preferred and actual working hours for spouse | −12.9 | −15.0 | −5.2 | −6.5 | −30.0 |
| **Transitional** | | | | | |
| Actual working hours | 36.7 | 43.5 | 60.0 | – | – |
| Preferred working hours for self | 55.7 | 40.0 | 40.0 | – | – |
| Difference between preferred and actual working hours for self | 19.0 | −3.5 | −20.0 | – | – |
| Spouse actual working hours | 19.5 | 40.0 | 0 | – | – |
| Preferred working hours for spouse | 40.0 | 30.0 | 20.0 | – | – |
| Difference between preferred and actual working hours for spouse | 20.5 | −10.0 | 20.0 | – | – |
| **Nontraditional** | | | | | |
| Actual working hours | 34.6 | 22.8 | 20.0 | 46.0 | 39.0 |
| Preferred working hours for self | 27.5 | 23.9 | 20.0 | 30.7 | 40.0 |
| Difference between preferred and actual working hours for self | −7.1 | 1.1 | 0 | −15.3 | 1.0 |
| Spouse actual working hours | 47.5 | 40.2 | 52.5 | 40.0 | 30.0 |
| Preferred working hours for spouse | 38.3 | 35.6 | 40.0 | 33.3 | 30.0 |
| Difference between preferred and actual working hours for spouse | −9.2 | −4.6 | −12.5 | −6.7 | 0 |

The Nontraditional men who were raised by parents with a more traditionally gendered division of housework seem interested in not mimicking their parents by desiring to spend relatively few hours in the labor market, possibly to facilitate their housework performance. Nontraditional men raised by Egalitarian parents seem to desire that they and their spouses work approximately the same hours, possibly to facilitate a more equal division of labor. It is possible that these desired shifts are the result of men's own preferences, but they could also indicate their spouses' exertion of latent power.

## Reports of disagreements

Without spousal reports, the data in Table 9.12 can be read as a partial window into whether spouses exert latent or hidden power in their verbal interactions. Among the female adult children, those in the Traditional class report more frequent disagreements than do women in the other two classes. The Nontraditional women report relatively low levels of disagreements, suggesting that they have been able to exert some amount of latent or hidden power in their marriage such that their expectations of behaviors are usually met. Without partner reports, we cannot confirm these relatively low levels of disagreements. Interestingly, Ultra-Traditional and Traditional women report similar levels of disagreements over the performance of housework. Recall that both of these classes are comprised of women who perform high levels of housework and do so in very gendered ways (that is, performing more of the traditionally feminine tasks). As these two classes were more likely than Nontraditional women to have been raised in a home (Table 9.5) that was Ultra-Traditional or Traditional, as well as to have seen their parents become more egalitarian in their division of

**Table 9.12:** Adult child class membership and reports of disagreements

| | Female adult children | | | Male adult children | | |
|---|---|---|---|---|---|---|
| | Ultra-Traditional | Trad-itional | Non-traditional | Trad-itional | Transi-tional | Non-traditional |
| *Respondent reports (%) of disagreement about:* | | | | | | |
| Household tasks | 34.3 | 33.9 | 17.9 | 21.4 | 28.6 | 26.7 |
| Money | 22.8 | 32.2 | 24.7 | 20.6 | 28.6 | 26.7 |
| Spending time together | 28.6 | 31.5 | 19.6 | 20.2 | 28.6 | 30.4 |
| Sex | 5.7 | 20.4 | 12.3 | 13.7 | 14.2 | 12.5 |
| In-laws | 17.1 | 22.1 | 17.4 | 10.3 | 28.6 | 19.6 |

housework over time (Table 9.6), the higher levels of disagreements may reflect their attempts at executing overt power to reduce their gendered burden.

There is a great similarity in the reports of disagreements among the male adult children, regardless of housework class membership. Where there is variation, men in the Traditional class report lower levels of disagreements. This lower frequency could be indicative of the men exerting latent and hidden power, thus yielding fewer disagreements as circumstances are more consistent with their expectations. These men were just as likely as other men (Table 9.5) to be raised in an Ultra-Traditional or Traditional home but were slightly more likely to watch their parents' division of labor become more egalitarian over time (Table 9.6). It is entirely reasonable that the Traditional men were responding to the negotiations between their parents and exerting additional latent power to prevent disagreements from occurring.

In Tables 9.13 and 9.14, we situate both the adult female and male children's reports of disagreements into the context of their and their parents' housework classes. As with preferred labor-market hours, these tables will allow us to identify general intergenerational patterns

**Table 9.13:** Parental housework class membership, female adult child class membership, and disagreements

| Respondent reports (%) of disagreement about: | Ultra-Traditional | Trad-itional | Transi-tional Husband | Egalitarian | Egalitarian High Workload |
|---|---|---|---|---|---|
| **Ultra-Traditional** | | | | | |
| Household tasks | 0 | 50.0 | 100.0 | – | – |
| Money | 0 | 16.7 | 100.0 | – | – |
| Spending time together | 0 | 16.7 | 100.0 | – | – |
| Sex | 0 | 0 | 100.0 | – | – |
| In-laws | 0 | 33.3 | 0 | – | – |
| **Traditional** | | | | | |
| Household tasks | 16.7 | 46.2 | 33.3 | 50.0 | 0 |
| Money | 16.7 | 46.2 | 33.3 | 50.0 | 0 |
| Spending time together | 66.7 | 23.1 | 33.3 | 0 | 50.0 |
| Sex | 16.7 | 23.1 | 0 | 50.0 | 0 |
| In-laws | 16.7 | 38.5 | 33.3 | 0 | 0 |
| **Nontraditional** | | | | | |
| Household tasks | 30.0 | 7.84 | 50.0 | 42.86 | 0 |
| Money | 40.0 | 17.7 | 25.0 | 28.6 | 16.7 |
| Spending time together | 30.0 | 17.7 | 37.5 | 28.6 | 0 |
| Sex | 20.0 | 11.8 | 0 | 42.9 | 0 |
| In-laws | 30.0 | 13.7 | 25.0 | 28.6 | 16.7 |

**Table 9.14:** Parental housework class membership, male adult child class membership, and disagreements

| Respondent reports (%) of disagreement about: | Ultra-Traditional | Trad-itional | Transitional Husband | Egalitarian | Egalitarian High Workload |
|---|---|---|---|---|---|
| **Traditional** | | | | | |
| Household tasks | 16.7 | 21.9 | 20.0 | 50.0 | 40.0 |
| Money | 16.7 | 28.1 | 20.0 | 16.7 | 40.0 |
| Spending time together | 16.7 | 21.9 | 40.0 | 33.3 | 0 |
| Sex | 25.0 | 12.5 | 20.0 | 0 | 20.0 |
| In-laws | 0 | 3.25 | 20.0 | 16.7 | 40.0 |
| **Transitional** | | | | | |
| Household tasks | 50.0 | 0 | 100.0 | – | – |
| Money | 50.0 | 0 | 100.0 | – | – |
| Spending time together | 50.0 | 0 | 0 | – | – |
| Sex | 25.0 | 0 | 100.0 | – | – |
| In-laws | 50.0 | 0 | 100.0 | – | – |
| **Nontraditional** | | | | | |
| Household tasks | 12.5 | 33.3 | 0 | 66.7 | 50.0 |
| Money | 12.5 | 26.7 | 0 | 66.7 | 0 |
| Spending time together | 37.5 | 40.0 | 50.0 | 66.7 | 50.0 |
| Sex | 25.0 | 20.0 | 0 | 0 | 0 |
| In-laws | 25.0 | 26.7 | 0 | 33.3 | 0 |

of how power may be exerted within households despite the small sample sizes in each of the child by parent housework class category. Table 6.3 documented that parents in the Egalitarian High Workload class reported the most frequent disagreements overall and those in the more traditionally gendered distribution classes reported the fewest. Here, we do see some patterns in behaviors as the more traditionally gendered performers of housework among the female and male children of more traditionally gendered housework performers report very few disagreements. The notable exceptions are Traditional adult women raised by Traditional parents disagreeing about household tasks and Traditional women raised by Ultra-Traditional parents disagreeing about spending time together. As there are few women in each group, we caution against making claims about those specific differences.

Overall, it seems that there is evidence of men with more traditional housework performance being able to exert power in order to have fewer disagreements in ways that also reflect an intergenerational transmission of conflict resolution tactics. Both women and men raised by couples marked by more traditionally gendered divisions of housework report fewer disagreements, suggesting that there is an intergenerational cultural roadmap that is comprised of traditional gendered norms and whether they are seen as problematic. The adult children who were raised in these more traditionally gendered homes may also have been more likely to partner with someone from a similar background, which is something that we cannot know from our data. However, the norms and values around the need to try to use disagreements as a mechanism to create change and thus reflect a desire to exert power (whether overt or latent) do seem to be transmitted intergenerationally based on the child by parent housework class analysis presented here.

## Summary

This chapter has demonstrated the long-standing influence of power dynamics and the household division of labor that was documented in one's household of origin during their formative years as it contributes to variation in overall work patterns both inside and outside of the home during adulthood. The most striking evidence of this transmission of behaviors is the response of adult children to the extent of change in their parents' housework class membership (and thus division of household labor) over the five years between Waves 1 and 2. Adult women needed to see negotiations in their parents' housework time in order to see a way forward that was not the path of least resistance of being in the Ultra-Traditional class themselves, though there remained a remarkable amount of cultural pressure for women to spend a substantial amount of time on traditionally feminine tasks. However, negotiations seemed to solidify the benefits of being in the Traditional class for men. As we expected, our results have documented how power dynamics are transmitted intergenerationally. Seeing negotiations (even toward a more traditional division of labor) empowers women to negotiate out of performing extraordinarily high amounts of housework (and thus being in our Ultra-Traditional class). Seeing negotiations challenges men's understanding of traditional power relations in heterosexual couples and discourages them from being willing to do more in their own homes. One caveat to this is the group of men whose parents became more traditional but were themselves in the Nontraditional class. Subsequent analysis showed that these men held the most gender-egalitarian attitudes of the adult men in the sample; their housework time was a reflection of their own beliefs.

The final chapter of this book (Chapter 10) provides a summary of the key findings from our analysis. We provide suggestions for how practitioners and other scholars can use our findings as they work with couples, critically assessing the implications of the changing cultural norms around relationships in the U.S. for our findings.

# 10

# Insights for helping families

## Introduction

The goal of this chapter is to help family scholars and practitioners working with couples by highlighting how our work can move both research and family support efforts forward. After summarizing our argument that housework performance provides a window into power dynamics in households and the empirical contributions that this book has made to evaluating that argument, we present potential implications of this work for both researchers and practitioners.

## Summary of key findings

We started this volume by asking "Why study housework?" Or, to paraphrase the title of this book, "Why does who cleans count?" In Chapter 1, we argued that by studying housework, we can learn something about relationships. Studying the negotiation and renegotiation of the division of household labor tells us about the exercise of three kinds of power—overt, latent, and hidden—and how inequalities and inequities in intimate relationships emerge and are maintained. We argue that a key contribution of this book is to present the argument for how housework can be seen as a proxy for household power dynamics.

Chapter 2 laid out four theoretical frameworks or perspectives that attempt to explain the division of household labor: two that are resource-based (time availability and bargaining theory) and two social-psychological/symbolic frameworks (gender ideology and economic dependence). A fundamental assumption of all four of these frameworks is that household labor is seen as undesirable by both women and men, and that both will attempt to minimize the amount of housework that they do. Consequently, women and men engage in various methods of exerting overt, latent, and hidden power to avoid doing housework. Importantly, this means that inequalities in the division of household labor reflect this exercise of power.

As the unique data that we used to empirically examine our claim that the division of housework can be seen as a proxy for household power dynamics was collected in the late 1980s–early 1990s in the U.S., we used Chapter 3 to provide some of the cultural and historical context that framed the lives of the couples. As readers of this volume may not have substantial familiarity with that time period, we see this introduction to the politics around families as important to contextualize the analysis of housework that was performed by couples during that time frame.

We began our empirical analyses in Chapter 4 by constructing an empirical typology of the division of housework. Our latent profile analyses (LPAs) combined information on the average amount of time spent by women and men on nine household tasks to reflect five classes: Ultra-Traditional, Traditional, Transitional Husbands, Egalitarian, and Egalitarian High Workload. These five classes represent five different patterns of the distribution of nine common household tasks. The classes represent not only varying amounts of time spent on housework, but also gendered dynamics in the kinds of tasks performed by women and men. For example, when men increased the amount of their housework contributions, they tended to begin with yardwork and car maintenance—traditionally masculine tasks. Furthermore, when men did perform feminine tasks, they usually cooked rather than cleaned. We also noted that in households where men performed relatively high levels of housework—particularly in the two egalitarian classes—women also increased their housework hours.

Our next step was to examine the five classes in light of the four theoretical frameworks that we introduced in Chapter 2. While, generally speaking, the characteristics of the five classes were consistent with the theoretical frameworks, there were some notable discrepancies. For example, we found that both women and men in the Transitional Husbands class had greater levels of material resources (earnings, education, and occupational prestige) than did those in the other four classes. We noticed that scores on our measure of gender ideology did not clearly differentiate between members of the five classes. There were members of couples in the Egalitarian and Egalitarian High Workload classes who held relatively traditional gender beliefs, and there were couples in the Ultra-Traditional and Traditional classes who held relatively egalitarian beliefs.

In Chapter 5, we also compared the five classes in terms of couple and spousal demographic characteristics to see how the classes differed. Some of our most interesting findings here were the characteristics of the Egalitarian High Workload class. Men in this class perform the fewest hours of paid work while the women earn the greatest percentage of household income of the five classes. We argued that if both men and women were able to adjust their paid and non-paid working hours to their own preferences without regard to gender, the resulting households might look a lot like the Egalitarian High Workload class.

Our next analyses began to focus in on the use of housework as a proxy for power dynamics. In Chapter 6, we compared two aspects of power in couples: first, the exercise of latent power to achieve a partner's preferred division of household and market labor; and, second, the use of overt power in terms of the physical or psychological manipulation of one's partner with regard to disagreements and physical violence.

We found evidence that spouses used latent power to determine the amount of time spent in the paid labor market. For example, Ultra-Traditional men seem to prefer a highly gendered division of paid and unpaid work very much in the traditional "separate spheres" model, with themselves as breadwinners and their wives as full-time homemakers. On the other hand, both spouses in the Transitional Husbands and Egalitarian High Workload classes prefer that wives work more hours. Interestingly, Egalitarian High Workload couples seem to prefer a reduction in men's paid labor hours. These couples seem to be moving toward de-gendering their allocation of market and non-market work time and it does not appear that these couples exercise latent power relative to market work time.

Shifting toward the issue of conflict in relationships, we found that the Egalitarian High Workload class reported the most overall disagreements while the Traditional class reported the fewest. This finding is consistent with the idea that while the Traditional class represents the cultural norm in terms of the gendered "separate spheres" ideology, the Egalitarian High Workload couples are on the "cutting edge" of a de-gendered society. In terms of conflict resolution, we found few differences across classes, though women in Ultra-Traditional couples seem to be more likely to keep their opinions to themselves, which may be an example of men employing power in their arguments. Intimate partner violence certainly represents the exercise of direct power in couple relationships. No clear pattern emerged here, though women in the Ultra-Traditional and Traditional classes were on the lower end of the frequency of physical arguments.

Our latent trajectory analysis presented in Chapter 7 reported that couples were more likely to change class membership than to stay the same. We saw evidence of the use of power in couples as documented by their transitions in class membership. Couples who became more traditional in their class membership over time were more likely to have women with low occupational prestige scores in Wave 1. Latent power was also demonstrated through the connection between the use of resources and ideology. We suspect that to reduce cognitive dissonance, couples with men who were relatively low earners and where women held more traditional ideologies than did their spouses became more traditional in their division of housework over time.

Next, we turned our attention to change over time, studying the couples and their class membership over the four- to seven-year interval between Waves 1 and 2 of the National Survey of Families and Households (NSFH). In Chapter 8, we found that there was substantial change in the direction of more egalitarian and less traditional divisions of labor; the Egalitarian High Workload class became the largest class (41.1 percent) in our data and the Ultra-Traditional class shrank to only 7.7 percent of the sample.

Certain background characteristics seemed to be associated with changes in class membership over time. For example, couples that became more traditional tended to be somewhat more diverse (with respect to race and ethnicity) than those who became more egalitarian. It is also the case that the women in couples who became more traditional had lower occupational prestige scores at Wave 1; the men in these couples tended to have lower incomes as well. It is possible that these relatively low-earning men did less housework as a gender-deviance neutralization technique in order to augment their status as breadwinners. Among the Ultra-Traditional class, there is evidence of men exercising power to get women to reduce their work hours—that is, to strengthen the men's position as breadwinners. On the other hand, we saw women in the Egalitarian class using their power to get men to reduce their paid labor hours while increasing their contributions to housework. Finally, in the Transitional Husbands class, we saw suggestions of women (as their relative incomes rose) using latent power to induce their husbands to reduce paid labor hours while modestly increasing their housework contributions. So, both men and women (in different situations) seemed to employ different forms of power to move toward a more desirable distribution of paid and unpaid labor, some in the direction of increasing traditionalism and others toward greater equality in housework. Notably, these changes occurred as the economy in the U.S. changed as well, with rapid growth in globalization alongside lower inflation and unemployment and a recession in 1990/91 (Gardner, 1994; Gamber and Hung, 2001; Reed, 2014).

Finally, in Chapter 9, we examined how the division of paid and unpaid labor in one's family of origin affected children in adulthood.

Here, we looked at the unpaid labor of the adult children of the NSFH couples as interviewed in 2001/02. We began by using LPA to create three classes for the women (Ultra-Traditional, Traditional, and Nontraditional) and three for the men (Traditional, Transitional, and Nontraditional). We used essentially the same techniques as we had used for their parents' housework data from Waves 1 and 2 examining the amount of time spent on the nine household tasks. There was weak but consistent evidence of the intergenerational transmission of housework norms for women; for example, women who were classified as Ultra-Traditional did not have parents from the Egalitarian or Egalitarian High Workload classes. However, there were no such patterns for men. We inferred that while seeing their parents' negotiations over the division of household labor empowered women to negotiate a more equitable division for themselves, a different pattern emerged for men. We think that seeing these negotiations by their parents challenged men's understanding of traditional power relations and led them away from more equitable housework arrangements in their own households. In addition, we found little evidence of the intergenerational transmission of the use of overt or latent power to shape preferred labor-market hours for either women or men, but there was some evidence that the housework class in which women and men were raised differentially influenced the use of disagreements as a way to exert power based upon the adult children's own housework class membership. Thus, we argue that the relationship between housework and power becomes part of the socialization process that is then played out across generations.

## Implications for practitioners

Of what value is it to understand that housework not only serves as a proxy for power dynamics in couples at one point in time, but can foretell changes in the economic decisions that couples may make in the future? Why is it important that we understand how power dynamics can be transmitted from parents to children? Family practitioners working with couples in the rapidly changing 21st century can benefit from our findings as they work to serve their clients.

### Insights into the changing demographics of the U.S.

The demographics of the U.S. are changing. Our results tell us how couples in the 1990s divided their labor but can also help us make predictions about couples of the 21st century. As the economy shifted in the early 1990s, and the couples in our sample aged, there was an increased likelihood of couples to distribute housework tasks in a more egalitarian manner. Some scholars have noted that a more egalitarian division of labor occurs as women gain greater economic influence in the home because women are using their income to purchase services to replace their labor (Gupta, 2006; Gupta and Ash, 2008). If that were occurring in our data, it would be evidence in support of our argument, in that women with greater power had the ability to shift the housework onto someone else. As the U.S. is greying, we could only expect some additional movement toward an egalitarian division of labor.

Examining the demographic distribution of couples in the Egalitarian High Workload class in Wave 1 shows us that they were far more likely to be persons of color than the other groups and that husbands in this class spent the least amount of time in paid work. This division of labor for the Egalitarian High Workload couples is suggestive of what couples could look like if both men and women are given the opportunity to pay equal attention to both paid and unpaid labor, both work and family lives.

It is also important to note the relatively high representation of non-white couples in the Transitional Husbands class in Wave 2. As those couples are comprised of men not quite performing housework at the Egalitarian class levels but more likely to perform feminine tasks than Traditional men, they (or younger versions of them) may be the couples of the future. By 2035, the U.S. is expected to have more older adults than children and immigration will be driving population growth (Vespa et al, 2018). Combined with evidence that women born in the 1990s expect their husbands to be (equal) contributors to the housework (Gerson, 2009), we can expect the 21st century to be comprised of more couples whose housework pattern would mirror the Transitional Husbands class found in our study. This is not without a concern. While women want their husbands to perform more housework, men continue to hold onto traditional ideals of what their married life will be (Gerson, 2009). Our data show that couples in the Transitional Husbands class are at a slightly higher risk of arguing heatedly and having a physical argument (perhaps performing gender-deviance neutralization). Therefore, there are implications from this changing demography of the U.S. for practitioners working with couples.

## Insights for working with couples

As couples in the U.S. will be simultaneously aging (and potentially becoming more egalitarian in their division of labor) and becoming more racially/ethnically diverse (and potentially comprised of men struggling with uncertain norms of masculinity), practitioners working with couples may find our work connecting housework and power dynamics useful. Changing norms of masculinity will likely pose a substantial challenge over the next few decades. How couples navigate those changes together will be reflected in their housework, labor-market participation, and overall relationship dynamics. Further, as couples age, their housework performance, labor-market participation, and overall relationship dynamics will also shift.

Counselors working with couples regularly introduce discussions about the division of housework into their sessions (Gottman, 1999; Ogletree et al, 2006). This information can not only be used to highlight expectations from both spouses regarding their roles within the family, but, based on our work, also provide insights into the potential subtle ways in which spouses are exerting power over one another. As we have documented some patterns of restricting (or encouraging) access to the labor market and conflict resolution tactics based upon the division of housework, we argue that practitioners counseling couples can use our work as another tool to assess potential risk within couples. As researchers and family sociologists, we are not qualified to tell counselors how to work with their clients. However, if our work can be used as a tool to aid counselors and other family practitioners to work with couples to become happier and healthier, then we would like to be able to contribute to that effort.

## Insights for family scholars

Previous research on housework has been remiss in not consistently framing the process being investigated as one that is about power. In the rush to document the inequality in specific households or any change over time, we researchers do not always highlight that the processes leading to inequality are reflections of power dynamics. While documenting inequality may make our research more palatable to the press and the general public, we are doing a disservice to everyone by underemphasizing the ways in which intimate relationships are negotiations of power just like other relationships. We cannot ignore the systemic ways in which U.S. culture privileges men; one piece of evidence of that privilege is the relative lack of men's performance of housework tasks, especially routine tasks. Power and privilege are intertwined in households, just as in other complex relationships, despite Americans' discomfort with moving beyond the idyllic expectations of what the family should be (Coontz, 1992).

Sociologists tend to study structural relationships and examine systematic patterns within groups rather than focusing on interpersonal or individual differences alone. Dialing back the rhetoric of power to make research palatable to the general public is counterproductive if one of the goals of sociologists in studying housework is to not only document inequality, but also work toward reducing it. As Treas and Drobnič (2010: 8) argue, we study housework (cross-nationally) because "by identifying the critical conditions that promote or impede gender parity in the family, cross-national comparisons of household labor can also inform policies to advance equality between women and men in society." Consequently, one immediate research pathway forward would be to follow Pesquera's (1993) lead and investigate interactions in other types of intimate relationships, including dating relationships, parent–child relationships, and close friendships, for factors leading to perceived power and dependency, as well as the conditions under which power is deployed. Our work has focused on married couples and cohabiting partners; much more can be learned from other intimate relationships as well.

Our findings highlight the value of using housework as a means to understand power dynamics in couples. However, our data are relatively old. Much has changed in the U.S. since the early 1990s when the Wave 2 data of the NSFH were collected and 2001/02 when the adult children data were collected. Marriage equality is the law in the U.S. as of 2015, meaning that individuals can legally marry someone of either the same or different sex. While research has investigated relationship dynamics in lesbian and gay couples (for an early study, see Carrington, 1999; for more recent scholarly inquiries, see Biblarz and Savci, 2010; Umberson et al, 2015; Goldberg and Romero, 2018), marriage equality as a law is still relatively new. Does the distribution of housework in lesbian and gay couples reflect the same type of power dynamics as in heterosexual couples once they are married? This is a conceptually rich line of inquiry as it will allow for a more nuanced development of the theoretical mechanisms at work in marriages in the contemporary U.S.

The Great Recession that occurred during 2007–09 was a global phenomenon. Research has noted that families responded to the economic crisis in ways that seem to reflect the softening of the connection between financial responsibility and gender (Mattingly and Smith, 2010; Davis et al, 2012). The generation that came of age in the midst of the Great Recession may approach marital roles and responsibilities differently given the tumultuous economic circumstances that evidenced the undermining of jobs across all occupational levels but especially among professional occupations (Goodman and Mance, 2011). Further investigation into whether and how the unstable global economy may influence personal educational and employment decisions, as well as couple dynamics, is warranted.

As we only followed couples who remained married over the two NSFH waves, we did not examine whether and how housework class membership shaped (or was shaped by) the likelihood of marital dissolution. Perceptions of fairness around housework are tied to marital quality and marital dissolution (Greenstein, 1996a; Lavee and Katz, 2002; Frisco and Williams, 2003). Therefore, it is likely that the power dynamics evidenced in the five classes over time did not reflect the kind of power used to end the relationship altogether. Our work may highlight the selective dynamics of couples for whom either divorce is not a religious or economic option, or the disagreements (which they did have [see Chapter 6]) were part of being a couple and thus did not warrant the response of relationship dissolution. It would be interesting to examine the longitudinal relationship between housework class and marital stability in the 21st century given the changes in marital and gender norms, as well as changes in the global economic system.

## Conclusion

Housework is more than simply doing the laundry, preparing meals, and mowing the grass. Housework is a reflection of individual preferences and negotiated expectations between partners, which are complicated by the expectations that others place upon women and men that are connected to how well they conform to gendered norms (West and Zimmerman, 1987; Berk, 1985). Our work has demonstrated that to understand the division of housework within heterosexual couples is to have insight into the power dynamics, both overt and hidden, within the couple. These power dynamics reflect the give and take of family life, where couples attempt to bring their beliefs, expectations, and behaviors into congruence. The reciprocal relationship between time in paid and unpaid tasks that is documented in this book highlights the value of studying housework to understand overt, latent, and hidden power. As families in the U.S. continue to construct and reconstruct their household-level norms amid changing geopolitical, cultural, and economic forces, one fact will still remain: household tasks will still need to be performed. Who cleans counts because cleaning and other household tasks highlight the potential for both women and men to be part of their ideal relationships, potentially yielding greater equality and/or happiness. We hope that our book can facilitate opportunities for both.

# Appendix

This book presents housework patterns for adults, and later their adult children, living in the U.S. in the late 20th and early 21st centuries. We present the results of a latent profile analysis (LPA) as a simplified way of understanding the patterns of how domestic labor has been performed in households, first by focusing on heterosexual couples and then by examining the housework reported by the adult children of those couples. We also examine class membership change over time among the couples in our sample through latent trajectory analysis (LTA).

## Constructing the five adult classes

### Data

To construct the five classes of housework performance, we used the National Survey of Families and Households (NSFH) (Sweet et al, 1988) Wave 1 data. This data set is an important one in the study of families as it includes survey information as completed by both partners in a relationship measuring behaviors and attitudes across a large spectrum. Our analytic data set was first constructed by including only couples (either married or cohabiting) for whom we had complete data on the housework measures for both partners ($N = 3,906$). We use the language of "women," "men," and "partners" in addition to "wives," "husbands," and "spouses" to highlight the inclusion of both married and cohabiting couples in the sample. Housework was measured by asking each partner about the number of hours per week that they typically performed each of the following tasks: meal preparation, kitchen work, cleaning, grocery shopping, doing laundry, paying bills, performing yardwork, performing car maintenance, and driving for the household. Responses to these questions were recoded to have maximum values at the 95th percentile for the range of the measure if respondents reported extremely high levels of housework in any task. This decision is consistent with how other researchers treat outliers using these data (for example, South and Spitze, 1994).

### LPA

We used LPA in Mplus (Muthén and Muthén, 1998–2017) to determine that there were five overall classes of couples based upon their distribution of housework task performance. As an analytic process, LPA, like latent class analysis (LCA), is designed to take large amounts of data and suggest fewer latent classes that represent key types of people in the population, allowing researchers the ability to assign each case in the data to one of those classes by estimating the probabilities of belonging to each class on the basis of the person's survey responses (Collins and Lanza, 2010). LPA uses continuous data, whereas LCA uses categorical data, to determine the hidden classes within the population. As there were nine measures of housework performance for each partner, our analysis relied upon 18 continuous measures of housework to determine the latent profiles within the sample.

As an analytic approach, LPA is well suited for this project as it reveals the existence of groups that differ substantively when membership in those groups is not known a priori and not easy to predict from any one indicator. Given the variety in types of housework tasks and that both women and men are potentially performing those tasks in varying amounts, LPA provides a window into the patterned behaviors across couples that other statistical methods would not.

Researchers rely on several criteria to determine class enumeration: theory, substantive meaning, and fit indices (Collins and Lanza, 2010). We examined six fit statistics to evaluate models: Vuong–Lo–Mendell–Rubin likelihood ratio test (VLMR); Lo–Mendell–Rubin likelihood ratio test (LMRT); Bayesian Information Criterion (BIC); Akaike Information Criterion (AIC); parametric bootstrapped likelihood ratio test (BLRT); and Entropy (Nylund et al, 2007; Asparouhov and Muthén, 2012). In instances where fit statistics did not agree on the best model, we relied on the recommendation by LCA and LPA experts to choose the number of latent classes based on the most conceptually defensible and meaningful model that is theoretically informed (Collins and Lanza, 2010; Foti et al, 2012).

Standard practice (Nylund et al, 2007; Morgan, 2015) is to choose the class enumeration model that has the lowest BIC value and/or the $k - 1$ number of classes once the LMRT (calculated via TECH 11) no longer has a statistically significant $p$-value. Conventionally, the lower the AIC, BIC, and adjusted BIC indices, the better the fit. Entropy reflects how distinct the classes are from one another; therefore, the higher the value, the better the fit. VLMR and BLRT compare the improvement in fit between neighboring class models, comparing $k - 1$ with $k$ class models. A significant $p$-value indicates that a $k$ class model is a better fit than the $k - 1$ model (Collins and Lanza, 2010). Our large sample size (3,906 couples) meant that over 190 stable classes of 5 percent of the sample (approximately 40 couples) could be potentially enumerated. Close investigation of the fit indices and actual distribution of the couples across the classes and housework measures led us to determine that the best fitting model that was also most consistent with previous theorizing was the five-class model that we present in Chapter 4 (Ultra-Traditional, Traditional, Transitional Husbands, Egalitarian, and Egalitarian High Workload). The rate of change in our BIC slowed substantially around the five-class model (compare the five-class and six-class models in Table A1), and while entropy is not a measure of model fit that should necessarily be relied upon to determine class enumeration, the five-class model Entropy value is the best among the multi-class solutions (beyond a two-class solution that is inconsistent with the literature). Given that the five-class model is also consistent with theorizing around couple relationship dynamics that was published around the time that the data were collected (for example, Hochschild and Machung, 1989), we felt comfortable proceeding with the five-class model as our description of the sample.

## Housework within each class

The five classes are profiles of groups of couples based upon how they divide the housework. The classes themselves are different from one another. Table A2 documents the average time spent on each task within each couple and the extent to which the time spent on each task by either the wife or husband differs across classes. We performed ANOVA tests and determined that there were significant differences in the performance of all tasks across the classes except for wives' performance of car maintenance. The final column notes the significant contrasts across classes for each task, with the numbers referencing the class numbers provided in parentheses with each class label.

**Table A1:** Model fit statistics used to determine class enumeration

| Classes | # Para-meters | AIC | BIC | BLRT p value | VLMR p value | LMRT p value | Entropy |
|---|---|---|---|---|---|---|---|
| 1 | 36 | 306,858.64 | 307,084.37 | – | – | – | – |
| 2 | 55 | 300,871.2 | 301,216.07 | 0.000 | 0.000 | 0.000 | 0.921 |
| 3 | 74 | 296,315.74 | 296,779.74 | 0.000 | 0.000 | 0.000 | 0.879 |
| 4 | 93 | 294,761.95 | 295,345.08 | 0.000 | 0.000 | 0.000 | 0.859 |
| 5 | 112 | 293,010.80 | 293,713.07 | 0.000 | 0.000 | 0.000 | 0.916 |
| 6 | 131 | 291,948.51 | 292,769.91 | 0.000 | 0.000 | 0.000 | 0.913 |

**Table A2:** Mean task performance comparison across classes

| | Ultra-Traditional (1) | Traditional (2) | Transitional Husbands (3) | Egalitarian (4) | Egalitarian High Workload (5) | Significant contrasts by class |
|---|---|---|---|---|---|---|
| **Wife task performance** | | | | | | |
| Meals | 16.96 | 7.49 | 7.96 | 7.03 | 9.01 | 1–5, 1–3, 1–2, 1–4, 5–2, 5–4, 3–4 |
| Kitchen | 14.64 | 5.62 | 6.42 | 6.23 | 7.80 | 1–5, 1–3, 1–4, 1–2, 5–3, 5–4, 5–2, 3–2, 4–2 |
| Cleaning | 14.42 | 5.85 | 6.12 | 7.14 | 7.40 | 1–5, 1–4, 1–3, 1–2, 5–2, 4–3, 4–2 |
| Groceries | 3.88 | 2.30 | 2.35 | 2.48 | 2.86 | 1–5, 1–4, 1–3, 1–2, 5–3, 5–2 |
| Laundry | 6.33 | 3.36 | 3.31 | 4.08 | 3.71 | 1–4, 1–5, 1–2, 1–3, 4–2, 4–3 |
| Bills | 2.13 | 1.27 | 1.34 | 1.50 | 1.89 | 7–5, 1–4, 1–3, 1–2, 5–4, 5–3, 5–2, 4–2 |
| Yardwork | 3.21 | 1.26 | 1.28 | 1.30 | 1.46 | 1–5, 1–4, 1–3, 1–2 |
| Car maintenance | 0.12 | 0.12 | 0.13 | 0.12 | 0.18 | No differences |
| Driving | 1.91 | 1.01 | 1.12 | 1.22 | 1.52 | 1–5, 1–4, 1–3, 1–2, 5–2 |
| **Husband task performance** | | | | | | |
| Meals | 1.10 | 1.38 | 2.96 | 6.96 | 7.86 | 5–4, 5–3, 5–2, 5–1, 4–3, 4–2, 4–1, 3–2, 3–1, 2–1 |
| Kitchen | 1.19 | 1.21 | 2.76 | 6.21 | 8.12 | 5–4, 5–3, 5–1, 5–2, 4–3, 4–1, 4–2, 3–1, 3–2 |
| Cleaning | 1.13 | 1.08 | 2.70 | 3.00 | 5.59 | 5–4, 5–3, 5–1, 5–2, 4–3, 4–1, 4–2, 3–1, 3–2 |
| Groceries | 1.21 | 1.07 | 1.86 | 2.35 | 3.34 | 5–4, 5–3, 5–1, 5–2, 4–3, 4–1, 4–2, 3–1, 3–2 |
| Laundry | 0.14 | 0.21 | 2.38 | 0.30 | 2.72 | 5–3, 5–4, 5–2, 5–1, 4–3, 4–2, 4–1, 3–2, 3–1, 2–1 |
| Bills | 1.23 | 1.05 | 1.39 | 1.61 | 2.12 | 5–4, 5–3, 5–1, 5–2, 4–2, 3–2, 1–4, 1–2 |
| Yardwork | 6.13 | 4.18 | 4.41 | 6.58 | 6.51 | 4–3, 4–2, 5–3, 5–2, 1–3, 1–2 |
| Car maintenance | 1.90 | 1.36 | 1.45 | 1.85 | 2.54 | 5–1, 5–4, 5–3, 5–2, 1–3, 1–2, 4–3, 4–2 |
| Driving | 1.05 | 0.78 | 1.11 | 1.30 | 2.19 | 5–4, 5–3, 5–1, 5–2, 4–2, 3–2, 1–2 |
| Prevalence | 0.204 | 0.526 | 0.114 | 0.109 | 0.046 | |
| N | 798 | 2054 | 447 | 426 | 181 | |

## Understanding who is in each class

In Chapters 5 and 6, we analyze the sample based upon the five classes (Ultra-Traditional, Traditional, Transitional Husbands, Egalitarian, and Egalitarian High Workload) and statistically describe each class. We first present profiles of each class based upon characteristics usually associated with power and then include general demographic information for the individuals and the couples.

We measure characteristics usually associated with power based on previous theoretical and empirical analysis of the division of housework, including employment hours, educational attainment in years, annual income (individual and household), wife's relative income, age, gender ideology, and occupational prestige. For partners who were unemployed/out of the labor force, their work hours, income, and occupational prestige were included as zero in the analysis. Gender ideology was the sum of six measures that asked respondents' level of agreement with the items ($\alpha = 0.68$ for women and $0.66$ for men), where higher values reflect more traditional responses. Examples of these measures include "Preschool children are likely to suffer if their mother is employed," "It is much better for everyone if the man earns the main living and the woman takes care of the home and family," and "If a husband and a wife both work full-time, they should share household tasks equally" (for more details on this measure, see Greenstein, 1990).

Demographic characteristics for individual partners included race and religious affiliation. Demographic characteristics for the couple include union status, number of children in the household, duration of the relationship, whether this was a first marriage for both husband and wife, region of the country, and whether they lived in a metropolitan area.

## Predicting class consequences

As many of the predictors of class consequences are also direct predictors of class membership (see Chapter 5), we chose to examine the role of class membership on outcomes using path analysis in Mplus (Muthén and Muthén, 1998–2017), as depicted in Figure 6.1. This modeling approach allows us to disentangle how some predictors, such as working hours, directly influence the outcome but also indirectly influence it through class membership.

Class membership is a set of categories, or a nominal variable. Muthén and Muthén (1998–2017) note that Mplus will treat any categorical mediating variable (such as class membership) as an underlying continuous latent response variable that relates to the observed variable via calculated thresholds. In terms of our models predicting class consequences, we are able to present omnibus results regarding whether there are differences in preferred labor-market hours, reports of disagreements, conflict resolution tactics, and intimate partner violence based upon class membership net of individual-level and couple-level characteristics, including those characteristics predicting class membership. While our analyses were performed by applying a robust weighted least squares estimator using a diagonal weight matrix (WLSMV) as the estimator and using the probit link, as are suggested by Muthén and Muthén (1998–2017), there is currently no way of calculating the regression coefficient by comparing the effect of being in the Ultra-Traditional class (or any of the other classes) to that of being in the reference group, the Traditional class. Therefore, all tables in Chapter 6 documenting multivariate findings report whether class membership overall significantly predicts class consequences. Table A3 presents the regression coefficient for housework class calculated by Mplus when predicting each outcome; we document the other variables included in the best fitting models that yielded each coefficient.

## Examining changes in class membership over time

LTA allows for an examination of the stability or change in housework class membership over time. Our LTA model, estimated using Mplus (Muthén and Muthén, 1998–2017), determined that there was sufficient longitudinal profile similarity for us to proceed with that assumption. In other words, we determined that there was minimal shift in the profile definition (which drew upon housework performance) over the five years between the data collections in Wave 1 and Wave 2.

In examining the change in class membership over time as connected to changes in characteristics associated with power, we also deployed the path-analytic approach. Models predicting whether changes in individual-level resources between Wave 1 and Wave 2 were significantly associated with Wave 1 class membership used the same modeling approach as those models examining whether there were housework class membership differences in the measures of class consequences, net of other individual-level and couple-level characteristics. All tables in Chapter 8 documenting multivariate findings report whether class membership overall significantly predicted

**Table A3:** Results of multivariate models predicting class consequences

| | Estimate of effect of class membership | Predictors results are net of: |
|---|---|---|
| **Preferred labor-market hours** | | |
| Woman's preferred working hours | 8.134* | Woman's education, woman's hours worked, man's education, woman's gender ideology, man's gender ideology, number of children |
| Difference between woman's preferred and actual working hours | 8.096* | Woman's hours worked, number of children, man's gender ideology, woman's gender ideology, man's educational attainment |
| Woman's preferred working hours for man | −0.086 | Woman's work hours, number of children, man's educational attainment, woman's relative income |
| Difference between preferred and actual working hours for man as reported by woman | 1.102* | Woman's work hours, number of children, man's educational attainment, woman's relative income |
| Man's preferred working hours | −0.005 | Woman's work hours, man's educational attainment, number of children, man's work hours |
| Difference between man's preferred and actual working hours | 0.457 | Woman's work hours, number of children, woman's relative income, woman's race and man's race, man's educational attainment |
| Man's preferred working hours for woman | 0.577* | Woman's work hours, number of children, man's educational attainment, man's race, man's gender ideology, woman's gender ideology |
| Difference between preferred and actual working hours for woman as reported by man | 0.812* | Man's work hours, number of children, woman's relative income, man's gender ideology, man's educational attainment, woman's educational attainment, man's race, man's gender ideology |
| **Reports of disagreements** | | |
| Woman's overall disagreement score | −0.309* | Woman's work hours, number of children, man's educational attainment, man's work hours, woman's gender ideology |

(continued)

**Table A3:** Results of multivariate models predicting class consequences (continued)

| | Estimate of effect of class membership | Predictors results are net of: |
|---|---|---|
| **Woman's reports (%) of disagreement about:** | | |
| Household tasks | −0.088* | Woman's educational attainment, man's educational attainment, woman's work hours, man's work hours, number of children, woman's gender ideology |
| Money | −0.112* | Woman's educational attainment, woman's work hours, man's work hours, number of children, man's educational attainment, woman's gender ideology |
| Spending time together | −0.034 | Man's educational attainment, man's work hours, woman's work hours, number of children, woman's gender ideology, man's race |
| Sex | −0.057 | Woman's educational attainment, man's educational attainment, man's working hours, woman's working hours, number of children, woman's relative income, man's race |
| Children | −0.070* | Man's educational attainment, woman's work hours, number of children, woman's gender ideology |
| In-laws | −0.116* | Woman's educational attainment, number of children, woman's work hours, man's work hours |
| Man's overall disagreement score | −0.304* | Woman's work hours, number of children, man's educational attainment, man's work hours, woman's gender ideology |
| **Man's reports (%) of disagreement about:** | | |
| Household tasks | −0.052 | Woman's educational attainment, number of children, woman's gender ideology |
| Money | −0.124* | Woman's educational attainment, number of children, woman's gender ideology, man's work hours, man's race |
| Spending time together | −0.078* | Woman's educational attainment, number of children, man's educational attainment, man's gender ideology |

(continued)

| | Estimate of effect of class membership | Predictors results are net of: |
|---|---|---|
| **Man's reports (%) of disagreement about (continued)** | | |
| Sex | −0.061 | Woman's educational attainment, number of children, man's educational attainment, woman's gender ideology, man's gender ideology |
| Children | −0.014 | Woman's educational attainment, number of children, woman's work hours, man's work hours |
| In-laws | −0.048 | Woman's educational attainment, number of children, man's educational attainment, woman's gender ideology, woman's relative income, woman's work hours |
| **Woman reports (%) of:** | | |
| Keeping opinions to self | −0.076* | Number of children, man's work hours, woman's work hours, man's educational attainment |
| Discussing disagreements calmly | −0.066* | Woman's educational attainment, number of children, man's work hours, woman's work hours, woman's gender ideology |
| Argue heatedly or shout at each other | 0.034 | Woman's educational attainment, number of children, man's work hours, woman's work hours, woman's gender ideology |
| End up hitting or throwing things at each other | 0.055 | Woman's educational attainment, woman's work hours |
| **Man reports (%) of:** | | |
| Keeping opinions to self | 0.004 | Man's work hours, woman's educational attainment, number of children |
| Discussing disagreements calmly | 0.004 | Woman's educational attainment, number of children, man's educational attainment, woman's gender ideology |
| Argue heatedly or shout at each other | −0.049 | Woman's educational attainment |
| End up hitting or throwing things at each other | −0.117 | Woman's educational attainment, number of children, man's educational attainment |

(continued)

**Table A3:** Results of multivariate models predicting class consequences (continued)

| | Estimate of effect of class membership | Predictors results are net of: |
|---|---|---|
| **Woman reports of:** | | |
| Physical argument in the last year (%) | 0.102* | Woman's work hours, man's work hours, woman's educational attainment, number of children |
| Number of fights woman hit, shoved, or threw things at man | 0.007 | Man's gender ideology, woman's relative income |
| Was man ever cut, bruised, or seriously injured in an argument? | −0.062 | No factors were significant |
| Number of fights man hit, shoved, or threw things at woman | −0.062 | Number of children, woman's educational attainment |
| Was woman ever cut, bruised, or seriously injured in an argument? | 0.090 | No factors were significant |
| **Man reports of:** | | |
| Physical argument in the last year (%) | 0.063 | Number of children, woman's educational attainment |
| Number of fights woman hit, shoved, or threw things at man | 0.048 | Number of children |
| Was man ever cut, bruised, or seriously injured in an argument? | 0.071 | Number of children |
| Number of fights man hit, shoved, or threw things at woman | −0.055 | Man's educational attainment, number of children |
| Was woman ever cut, bruised, or seriously injured in an argument? | 0.025 | Man's educational attainment |

Note: *$p < .05$.

changes in individual-level resources, as well as whether changes in individual-level resources significantly predicted whether couples' class membership became more egalitarian, more traditional, or stayed the same over time and Wave 2 class membership. Table A4 presents the regression coefficients for housework class that were calculated by Mplus when predicting each measure of change in individual-level resources, Table A5 presents coefficients for models predicting change in housework class membership over time, and Table A6 predicts Wave 2 class membership based upon changes in individual-level characteristics. Measures of change in individual resources were included in models independently rather than all simultaneously. This modeling strategy allowed us to examine the extent to which there was an independent influence of each resource change on class

**Table A4:** Results of multivariate models predicting changes in individual-level resources

| Resource | Estimate of effect of Wave 1 class membership | Predictors results are net of: |
|---|---|---|
| Change in woman's average weekly work hours | −0.483 | Number of children, woman's work hours, man's work hours, woman's relative income, woman's gender ideology, man's gender ideology |
| Change in man's average weekly work hours | −1.634* | Number of children, man's gender ideology, woman's work hours, man's work hours, woman's gender ideology |
| Change in woman's earnings ($) | 0.053 | Number of children, man's gender ideology, woman's work hours, woman's relative income |
| Change in man's earnings ($) | 0.005 | Number of children, man's gender ideology, man's working hours, woman's working hours, woman's relative income |
| Change in woman's relative income (%) | 0.115* | Number of children, man's gender ideology, man's work hours, woman's work hours, woman's relative income, woman's gender ideology |
| Change in woman's occupational prestige | 0.024 | Number of children |
| Change in man's occupational prestige | −0.008 | Number of children, woman's gender ideology |
| Change in woman's relative occupational prestige (%) | −0.005 | Number of children, woman's working hours |

Note: *$p$ <.05.

membership change and Wave 2 class membership, as well as whether each change in resources was independently associated with Wave 1 class membership. The measures of change for all but working hours were included in the models as standardized variables, with a mean of 0 and standard deviation of 1 to reduce the variance of each measure and allow for the Mplus estimators to successfully complete the analyses. In each table, we also document the other variables included in the best fitting models that yielded each coefficient.

The coefficients in Table A5 should be interpreted as the influence of a greater positive change in a resource on the likelihood that the couple would become more traditional in their class membership over time.

The coefficients in Table A6 should be interpreted as the influence of a greater positive change in a resource on the likelihood that the couple would be classified as Traditional in Wave 2 relative to other classes.

**Table A5:** Results of multivariate models predicting changes in housework class membership over time

| Resource | Estimate of effect of resource | Predictors results are net of |
|---|---|---|
| Change in woman's average weekly work hours | 0.000 | Number of children, woman's relative income |
| Change in man's average weekly work hours | −0.004* | Wave 1 housework class, woman's relative income |
| Change in woman's earnings ($) | −0.074* | Man's gender ideology, woman's work hours, woman's relative income |
| Change in man's earnings ($) | −0.027 | Man's work hours, woman's relative income |
| Change in woman's relative income (%) | −0.032 | Woman's work hours, Wave 1 housework class, woman's gender ideology |
| Change in woman's occupational prestige | 0.073 | Woman's gender ideology |
| Change in man's occupational prestige | 0.121* | Woman's gender ideology |
| Change in woman's relative occupational prestige (%) | 0.004 | Number of children |

Note: *$p$ <.05.

146

**Table A6:** Results of multivariate models predicting Wave 2 housework class membership

| Resource | Estimate of effect of resource | Predictors results are net of |
|---|---|---|
| Change in woman's average weekly work hours | 0.010* | Number of children, woman's work hours man's work hours, woman's relative income |
| Change in man's average weekly work hours | −0.002 | Woman's work hours, man's work hours, woman's gender ideology, Wave 1 housework class, woman's relative income |
| Change in woman's earnings ($) | 0.156* | Woman's work hours, woman's relative income |
| Change in man's earnings ($) | 0.013* | Woman's work hours, man's work hours, number of children, woman's relative income |
| Change in woman's relative income (%) | 0.108* | Woman's work hours, man's work hours, woman's relative income, Wave 1 housework class |
| Change in woman's occupational prestige | −0.109* | Woman's work hours, woman's relative income |
| Change in man's occupational prestige | −0.241* | Woman's gender ideology, woman's relative income |
| Change in woman's relative occupational prestige (%) | 0.130* | Woman's relative income |

Note: *$p$ <.05.

## Determining adult children's class membership

Wave 3 of the NSFH provided information collected from the adult children of the NSFH respondents. We analyzed reported housework performance data from 260 female and 187 male children of the respondents included in our LPA analysis. As the children were asked to report the number of hours that they spent on each of the same nine tasks for which we had data on their parents (though we did not have data on their partners/spouses), we performed LPA on the women and men separately. Table A7 presents the model fit statistics for the LPA analysis of the adult female children's data while Table A8 presents model fit statistics for the LPA analysis of the adult male children's data.

The LPA results demonstrated that a three-class model best fit both the women's and men's data. For both women and men, as was the case for their parents, the classes are distinct from one another. Table A9 documents the average time spent on each task for the

**Table A7:** Model fit statistics used to determine class enumeration for female children

| Classes | # Parameters | AIC | BIC | BLRT p value | VLMR p value | LMRT p value | Entropy |
|---|---|---|---|---|---|---|---|
| 1 | 18 | 9,839.46 | 9,903.55 | – | – | – | – |
| 2 | 28 | 9,387.34 | 9,487.03 | 0.000 | 0.015 | 0.016 | 0.942 |
| 3 | 38 | 9,238.16 | 9,373.47 | 0.000 | 0.008 | 0.009 | 0.899 |
| 4 | 48 | 9,091.90 | 9,262.81 | 0.000 | 0.802 | 0.807 | 0.979 |

**Table A8:** Model fit statistics used to determine class enumeration for male children

| Classes | # Parameters | AIC | BIC | BLRT p value | VLMR p value | LMRT p value | Entropy |
|---|---|---|---|---|---|---|---|
| 1 | 18 | 6,708.61 | 6,766.76 | – | – | – | – |
| 2 | 28 | 6,392.04 | 6,482.50 | 0.000 | 0.000 | 0.000 | 0.896 |
| 3 | 38 | 6,247.80 | 6,370.58 | 0.000 | 0.013 | 0.014 | 0.943 |
| 4 | 48 | 6,179.01 | 6,334.10 | 0.000 | 0.133 | 0.139 | 0.954 |

**Table A9:** Mean task performance comparison across classes for female children

| | Ultra-Traditional (1) | Traditional (2) | Nontraditional (3) | Significant contrasts by class |
|---|---|---|---|---|
| Meals | 9.944 | 6.516 | 3.001 | 1–2, 1–3, 2–3 |
| Kitchen | 8.333 | 5.422 | 2.14 | 1–2, 1–3, 2–3 |
| Cleaning | 18.111 | 7.219 | 2.398 | 1–2, 1–3, 2–3 |
| Groceries | 3.944 | 2.578 | 1.461 | 1–2, 1–3, 2–3 |
| Laundry | 7.222 | 4.453 | 1.831 | 1–2, 1–3, 2–3 |
| Bills | 2.166 | 1.656 | 1.264 | 1–3, 2–3 |
| Yardwork | 2.18 | 2.031 | 1.808 | 1–2, 1–3, 2–3 |
| Car maintenance | 0.224 | 0.156 | 0.365 | No significant differences |
| Driving | 3.897 | 1.812 | 0.808 | 2–3 |
| Prevalence | 0.07 | 0.25 | 0.68 | |
| N | 18 | 64 | 178 | |

Note: All significant contrasts were significant for both Tukey and Bonferroni tests.

female children (and Table A10 for male children) across classes. We performed ANOVA tests and determined that there were significant differences in the performance of all tasks across the classes except for the performance of car maintenance. The final column notes the significant contrasts across classes for each task, where the numbers reference the class numbers provided in parentheses with each class label.

**Table A10:** Mean task performance comparison across classes for male children

| | Traditional (1) | Transitional (2) | Nontraditional (3) | Significant contrasts by class |
|---|---|---|---|---|
| Meals | 2.905 | 3.357 | 6.446 | 1–3, 2–3 |
| Kitchen | 2.025 | 2.928 | 5.464 | 1–3, 2–3 |
| Cleaning | 2.068 | 4.428 | 6.482 | 1–2, 1–3, 2–3 |
| Groceries | 1.316 | 1.214 | 2.553 | 1–3, 2–3 |
| Laundry | 1.41 | 1.642 | 3.357 | 1–3, 2–3 |
| Bills | 1.077 | 0.785 | 1.821 | 1–3, 2–3 |
| Yardwork | 1.709 | 3.428 | 2.107 | 1–3, 2–3 |
| Car maintenance | 0.324 | 3.998 | 0.339 | No significant differences |
| Driving | 0.41 | 0.214 | 2.017 | 1–2, 2–3 |
| Prevalence | 0.63 | 0.07 | 0.30 | |
| N | 117 | 14 | 56 | |

Note: All significant contrasts were significant for both Tukey and Bonferroni tests.

## Understanding who is in each class among the adult children

In Chapter 9, we analyze the sample of adult children of the couples included in our original NSFH sample. We statistically describe each of the three classes for the women (Ultra-Traditional, Traditional, and Nontraditional) and the men (Traditional, Transitional, and Nontraditional). We first present profiles of each class based upon characteristics usually associated with power and then include general demographic information for the individuals and the couples in a manner similar to the presentation of the profiles for the NSFH couples.

As with their parents, we measure characteristics usually associated with power based on previous theoretical and empirical analysis of the division of housework, including employment hours, educational attainment in years, individual annual income, wife's relative income and education, and gender ideology. The adult children in the analysis are married but we do not have self-reported measures from the adult children's spouses. All spousal measures are derived from the survey responses of the adult children. For adult children or their spouses who were unemployed/out of the labor force, their work hours and income were included as zero in the analysis. Gender ideology was the sum of five measures that asked respondents' level of agreement with the items ($\alpha = 0.58$ for women and $0.57$ for men), where higher values reflect more traditional responses. Examples of these items include "It is much better for everyone if the man earns the main living and the woman takes care of the home and family," "Preschool children are likely to suffer if their mother is employed," and "Both the husband and wife should contribute to family income."

Demographic characteristics for the adult children included race and religious affiliation. Demographic characteristics for the couple include marital duration and number of children under the age of five in the household.

# Notes

## Chapter 1

[1] For various reasons, researchers usually treat childcare and housework as two separate issues; while everyone has to deal with cooking, cleaning, and laundry, only parents have to deal with childcare, and the social support for men doing childcare is much more widespread than that for men doing housework.

## Chapter 8

[1] While there were a few outliers where the wives earned over $65,000, the trend of increased income despite decreased working hours and lower occupational prestige was stable when the analysis was performed without those couples. Therefore, we have continued to include those couples in our sample.

# References

Aassve, A., Fuochi, G., and Mencarini, L. (2014) Desperate housework relative resources, time availability, economic dependency, and gender ideology across Europe. *Journal of Family Issues*, 35(8): 1000–22.

Álvarez, B. and Miles-Touya, D. (2012) Exploring the relationship between parents' and children's housework time in Spain. *Review of Economics of the Household*, 10(2): 299–318.

Arrighi, B.A. and Maume, D.J. (2000) Workplace subordination and men's avoidance of housework. *Journal of Family Issues*, 21(4): 464–87.

Asparouhov, T. and Muthén, B. (2012) Using Mplus TECH11 and TECH14 to test the number of latent classes. Mplus Web Notes, No. 14. http://www.statmodel.com/examples/webnotes/webnote14.pdf

Atkinson, M.P., Greenstein, T.N., and Lang, M.M. (2005) For women, breadwinning can be dangerous: gendered resource theory and wife abuse. *Journal of Marriage and Family*, 67(5): 1137–48.

Bair-Merritt, M.H., Shea Crowne, S., Thompson, D.A., Sibinga, E., Trent, M., and Campbell, J. (2010) Why do women use intimate partner violence? A systematic review of women's motivations. *Trauma, Violence, & Abuse*, 11(4): 178–89.

Batalova, J.A. and Cohen, P.N. (2002) Premarital cohabitation and housework: couples in cross-national perspective. *Journal of Marriage and Family*, 64(3): 743–55.

Baxter, J. (1992) Power attitudes and time: the domestic division of labour. *Journal of Comparative Family Studies*, 23(2): 165–82.

Baxter, J. and Hewitt, B. (2013) Negotiating domestic labor: women's earnings and housework time in Australia. *Feminist Economics*, 19(1): 29–53.

Becker, G.S. (1981) *A treatise on the family*. Cambridge, MA: Harvard University Press.

Benjamin, O. and Sullivan, O. (1996) The importance of difference: conceptualising increased flexibility in gender relations at home. *Sociological Review*, 44: 225–51.

Benjamin, O. and Sullivan, O. (1999) Relational resources, gender consciousness and possibilities of change in marital relationships. *Sociological Review*, 47: 794–820.

Berk, S.F. (1985) *The gender factory: The apportionment of work in American households*. New York, NY: Plenum Press.

Bertrand, M., Kamenica, E., and Pan, J. (2013) Gender identity and relative income within households. NBER Working Paper 19023, National Bureau of Economic Research, Cambridge, MA.

Bianchi, S.M. and Milkie, M.A. (2010) Work and family research in the first decade of the 21st century. *Journal of Marriage and the Family*, 72(3): 705–25.

Bianchi, S.M., Milkie, M.A., Sayer, L.C., and Robinson, J.P. (2000) Is anyone doing the housework? Trends in the gender division of household labor. *Social Forces*, 79(1): 191–228.

Biblarz, T.J. and Savci, E. (2010) Lesbian, gay, bisexual, and transgender families. *Journal of Marriage and Family*, 72(3): 480–97.

Bittman, M., England, P., Folbre, N., Sayer, L., and Matheson, G. (2003) When does gender trump money? Bargaining and time in household work. *American Journal of Sociology*, 109(1): 186–214.

Blair, S.L. and Lichter, D.T. (1991) Measuring the division of household labor: gender segregation of housework among American couples. *Journal of Family Issues*, 12(1): 91–113.

Blood, R.O. and Wolfe, D.M. (1960) *Husbands and wives: The dynamics of married living.* New York, NY: Free Press.

Bolzendahl, C.I. and Myers, D.J. (2004) Feminist attitudes and support for gender equality: opinion change in women and men, 1974–1998. *Social Forces*, 83(2): 759–89.

Brayfield, A.A. (1992) Employment resources and housework in Canada. *Journal of Marriage and the Family*, 54(1): 19–30.

Brines, J. (1994) Economic dependency, gender, and the division of labor at home. *American Journal of Sociology*, 100(3): 652–88.

Carrington, C. (1999) *No place like home: Relationships and family life among lesbians and gay men.* Chicago, IL: University of Chicago Press.

Chafetz, J.S. (1988) The gender division of labor and the reproduction of female disadvantage—toward an integrated theory. *Journal of Family Issues*, 9(1): 108–31.

Collins, L.M. and Lanza, S.T. (2010) *Latent class and latent transition analysis: With applications in the social, behavioral, and health sciences.* New York, NY: Wiley.

Coltrane, S. (2000) Research on household labor: modeling and measuring the social embeddedness of routine family work. *Journal of Marriage and the Family*, 62(4): 1208–33.

Coltrane, S. and Ishii-Kuntz, M. (1992) Men's housework: a life course perspective. *Journal of Marriage and the Family*, 54(1): 43–57.

Connell, R.W. (1987) *Gender and power: Society, the person, and sexual politics.* Stanford, CA: Stanford University Press.

Coontz, S. (1992) *The way we never were: American families and the nostalgia trap*. New York, NY: Basic Books.

Coontz, S. (2006) *Marriage, a history: How love conquered marriage*. New York, NY: Penguin Books.

Cunningham, M. (2001) Parental influences on the gendered division of housework. *American Sociological Review*, 66(2): 184–203.

Cunningham, M. (2005) Gender in cohabitation and marriage—the influence of gender ideology on housework allocation over the life course. *Journal of Family Issues*, 26(8): 1037–61.

Daly, K.J. (2002) Time, gender, and the negotiation of family schedules. *Symbolic Interaction*, 25: 323–42.

Davis, S.N. (2010) Is justice contextual? Married women's perceptions of fairness of the division of household labor in 12 nations. *Journal of Comparative Family Studies*, 41(1): 19–41.

Davis, S.N. and Greenstein, T.N. (2009) Gender ideology: components, predictors, and consequences. *Annual Review of Sociology*, 35: 87–105.

Davis, S.N., Greenstein, T.N., and Marks, J.P.G. (2007) Effects of union type on division of household labor—do cohabiting men really perform more housework? *Journal of Family Issues*, 28(9): 1246–72.

Davis, S.N., Jacobsen, S.K., and Anderson, J. (2012) From the Great Recession to Greater gender equality? Family mobility and the intersection of race, class, and gender. *Marriage & Family Review*, 48(7): 601–20.

DeMaris, A. and Longmore, M.A. (1996) Ideology, power, and equity: testing competing explanations for the perception of fairness in household labor. *Social Forces*, 74(3): 1043–71.

DeVault, M.L. (1990) Conflict over housework: a problem that (still) has no name. *Research in Social Movements, Conflicts and Change*, 12: 189–202.

Emerson, R.M. (1962) Power-dependence relations. *American Sociological Review*, 27: 31–41.

Emerson, R.M. (1972a) Exchange theory, part I: a psychological basis for social exchange. In J. Berger, M. Zelditch Jr, and B. Anderson (eds) *Sociological theories in progress* (vol 2). Boston, MA: Houghton Mifflin, pp 38–57.

Emerson, R.M. (1972b) Exchange theory, part II: exchange relations and network structures. In J. Berger, M. Zelditch Jr, and B. Anderson (eds) *Sociological theories in progress* (vol 2). Boston, MA: Houghton Mifflin, pp 58–87.

England, P. (2011) Missing the big picture and making much ado about almost nothing: recent scholarship on gender and household work. *Journal of Family Theory & Review*, 3: 23–6.

England, P. and Folbre, N. (2005) Gender and economic sociology. In N.J. Smelser and R. Swedberg (eds) *The handbook of economic sociology*. Princeton, NJ: Princeton University Press, pp 627–49.

Evertsson, M. and Nermo, M. (2004) Dependence within families and the division of labor: comparing Sweden and the United States. *Journal of Marriage and Family*, 66(5): 1272–86.

Foti, R.J., Bray, B.C., Thompson, N.J., and Allgood, S.F. (2012) Know thy self, know thy leader: contributions of a pattern-oriented approach to examining leader perceptions. *The Leadership Quarterly*, 23: 702–17.

Frisco, M.L. and Williams, K. (2003) Perceived housework equity, marital happiness, and divorce in dual-earner households. *Journal of Family Issues*, 24(1): 51–73.

Gamber, E.N. and Hung, J.H. (2001) Has the rise in globalization reduced US inflation in the 1990s? *Economic Inquiry*, 39(1): 58–73.

Gardner, J.M. (1994) The 1990–91 recession: how bad was the labor market? In *Monthly Labor Review*. Washington, DC: Bureau of Labor Statistics.

Gazso-Windle, A. and McMullin, J.A. (2003) Doing domestic labour: strategising in a gendered domain. *Canadian Journal of Sociology—Cahiers Canadiens De Sociologie*, 28(3): 341–66.

Gerson, K. (2009) *The unfinished revolution: Coming of age in a new era of gender, work, and family*. New York, NY: Oxford University Press.

Goffman, E. (1977) The arrangement between the sexes. *Theory and Society*, 4(3): 301–31.

Goldberg, A.E. and Romero, A.P. (2018) *LGBTQ divorce and relationship dissolution: Psychological and legal perspectives and implications for practice*. New York, NY: Oxford University Press.

Goodman, C.J. and Mance, S.M. (2011) Employment loss and the 2007–09 recession: an overview. In *Monthly Labor Review*. Washington, DC: Bureau of Labor Statistics.

Gottman, J.M. (1999) *The marriage clinic: A scientifically-based marital therapy*. New York, NY: WW Norton & Company.

Greenstein, T.N. (1990) Marital disruption and the employment of married women. *Journal of Marriage and the Family*, 52(3): 657–76.

Greenstein, T.N. (1996a) Gender ideology and perceptions of the fairness of the division of household labor: effects on marital quality. *Social Forces*, 74(3): 1029–42.

Greenstein, T.N. (1996b) Husbands' participation in domestic labor: interactive effects of wives' and husbands' gender ideologies. *Journal of Marriage and the Family*, 58(3), 585–95.

Greenstein, T.N. (2000) Economic dependence, gender, and the division of labor in the home: a replication and extension. *Journal of Marriage and Family*, 62(2): 322–35.

Greenstein, T.N. (2009) National context, family satisfaction, and fairness in the division of household labor. *Journal of Marriage and the Family*, 71(4): 1039–51.

Gupta, S. (2006) Her money, her time: women's earnings and their housework hours. *Social Science Research*, 35(4): 975–99.

Gupta, S. (2007) Autonomy, dependence, or display? The relationship between married women's earnings and housework. *Journal of Marriage and Family*, 69(2): 399–417.

Gupta, S. and Ash, M. (2008) Whose money, whose time? A nonparametric approach to modeling time spent on housework in the United States. *Feminist Economics*, 14(1): 93–120.

Hattery, A. (2008) *Intimate partner violence*. Lanham, MD: Rowman & Littlefield.

Hochschild, A. and Machung, A. (1989) *The second shift*. New York, NY: Viking.

Hu, C.Y. and Kamo, Y. (2007) The division of household labor in Taiwan. *Journal of Comparative Family Studies*, 38(1): 105–24.

Kan, M.Y. (2008) Does gender trump money? Housework hours of husbands and wives in Britain. *Work, Employment and Society*, 22(1): 45–66.

Kilbourne, B.S., England, P., Farkas, G., Beron, K., and Weir, D. (1994). Returns to skill, compensating differentials, and gender bias: effects of occupational characteristics on the wages of white women and men. *American Journal of Sociology*, 100(3), 689–719.

Killewald, A. (2011) Opting out and buying out: wives' earnings and housework time. *Journal of Marriage and Family*, 73(2): 459–71.

Killewald, A. and Gough, M. (2010) Money isn't everything: wives' earnings and housework time. *Social Science Research*, 39(6): 987–1003.

Kluwer, E.S. (2011) Psychological perspectives on gender deviance neutralization. *Journal of Family Theory & Review*, 3: 14–17.

Kluwer, E.S., Heesink, J.A.M., and Van de Vliert, E. (1996) Marital conflict about the division of household labor and paid work. *Journal of Marriage and the Family*, 58(4): 958–69.

Kluwer, E.S., Heesink, J.A.M., and Van de Vliert, E. (1997) The marital dynamics of conflict over the division of labor. *Journal of Marriage and the Family*, 59(3): 635–53.

Kluwer, E.S., Heesink, J.A.M., and Van de Vliert, E. (2002) The division of labor across the transition to parenthood: a justice perspective. *Journal of Marriage and Family*, 64(4): 930–43.

Kolpashnikova, K. (2018) American househusbands: new time use evidence of gender display, 2003–2016. *Social Indicators Research*, 140(3), 1259–77.

Konigsberg, R.D. (2011) Chore wars. *Time*, 178(5): 44–9.

Lachance-Grzela, M. and Bouchard, G. (2010) Why do women do the lion's share of housework? A decade of research. *Sex Roles*, 63(11/12): 767–80.

Lavee, Y. and Katz, R. (2002) Division of labor, perceived fairness, and marital quality: the effect of gender ideology. *Journal of Marriage and Family*, 64(1): 27–39.

Lewin-Epstein, N., Stier, H., and Braun, M. (2006) The division of household labor in Germany and Israel. *Journal of Marriage and the Family*, 68(5): 1147–64.

Lorber, J. (2005) *Breaking the bowls: Degendering and feminist change.* New York, NY: Norton.

Lukes, S. (2005) *Power: A radical view* (2nd edn). New York, NY: Palgrave Macmillan.

Major, B. (1987) Gender, justice, and the psychology of entitlement. In P. Shaver and C. Hendrick (eds) *Review of personality and social psychology*, (vol. 7). Sex and gender (pp. 124–48). Thousand Oaks, CA: Sage.

Mattingly, M.J. and Smith, K.E. (2010) Changes in wives' employment when husbands stop working: a recession–prosperity comparison. *Family Relations*, 59(4): 343–57.

Morgan, G.B. (2015) Mixed mode latent class analysis: an examination of fit index performance for classification. *Structural Equation Modeling: A Multidisciplinary Journal*, 22: 76–86.

Muthén, L.K. and Muthén, B.O. (1998–2017) *Mplus user's guide, eighth edition.* Los Angeles, CA: Muthén & Muthén.

Nitsche, N. and Grunow, D. (2016) Housework over the course of relationships: gender ideology, resources, and the division of household labor from a growth curve perspective. *Advances in Life Course Research*, 29: 80–94.

Nordenmark, M. (2004) Does gender ideology explain differences between countries regarding the involvement of women and of men in paid and unpaid work? *International Journal of Social Welfare*, 13(3): 233–43.

Nordenmark, M. and Nyman, C. (2003) Fair or unfair? Perceived fairness of household division of labour and gender equality among women and men—the Swedish case. *European Journal of Women's Studies*, 10(2): 181–209.

Nylund, K.L., Asparouhov, T., and Muthén, B. (2007) Deciding on the number of classes in latent class analysis and growth mixture modeling. A Monte Carlo simulation study. *Structural Equation Modeling*, 14: 535–69.

Ogletree, S.M., Worthen, J.B., Turner, G.M., and Vickers, V. (2006) Developing an attitudes toward housecleaning scale: gender comparisons and counseling applications. *The Family Journal*, 14(4): 400–7.

Pesquera, B.M. (1993) "In the beginning he wouldn't lift even a spoon": the division of household labor. In A. de la Torre and B.M. Pesquera (eds) *Building with our hands: New directions in Chicana studies*. Berkeley, CA: University of California Press, pp 181–95.

Pimentel, E.E. (2006) Gender ideology, household behavior, and backlash in urban China. *Journal of Family Issues*, 27(3): 341–65.

Reed, S. (2014) One hundred years of price change: the Consumer Price Index and the American inflation experience. In *Monthly Labor Review*. Washington, DC: U.S. Bureau of Labor Statistics.

Reynolds, J. (2003) You can't always get the hours you want: mismatches between actual and preferred work hours in the U.S. *Social Forces*, 81(4): 1171–99.

Risman, B.J. (2009) From doing to undoing: gender as we know it. *Gender & Society*, 23: 81–4.

Risman, B.J. (2011) Gender as structure or trump card? *Journal of Family Theory & Review*, 3: 18–22.

Roof, W.C. and Hoge, D.R. (1980) Church involvement in America: social factors affecting membership and participation. *Review of Religious Research*, 21(4), 405–426.

Rubin, L.B. (1976) *Worlds of pain: Life in the working-class family*. New York, NY: Basic Books.

Sayer, L.C. (2005) Gender, time and inequality: trends in women's and men's paid work, unpaid work and free time. *Social Forces*, 84(1): 285–303.

Schneider, D. (2011) Market earnings and household work: new tests of gender performance theory. *Journal of Marriage and Family*, 73(4): 845–60.

Schneider, D. (2012) Gender deviance and household work: the role of occupation. *American Journal of Sociology*, 117(4): 1029–72.

Shelton, B.A. and John, D. (1996) The division of household labor. *Annual Review of Sociology*, 22: 299–322.

South, S.J. and Spitze, G. (1994) Housework in marital and nonmarital households. *American Sociological Review*, 59(3), 327–347.

Straus, M.A. (1979) Measuring intra-family conflict and violence—conflict tactics (CT) scales. *Journal of Marriage and the Family*, 41(1): 75–88.

Sullivan, O. (2006) *Changing gender relations, changing families: Tracing the pace of change over time*. Lanham, MD: Rowman & Littlefield.

Sullivan, O. (2011) An end to gender display through the performance of housework? A review and reassessment of the quantitative literature using insights from the qualitative literature. *Journal of Family Theory & Review*, 3: 1–13.

Sweet, J., Bumpass, L., and Call, V. (1988) *The design and content of the National Survey of Families and Households*. Madison, WI: Center for Demography and Ecology.

Thébaud, S. (2010) Masculinity, bargaining and breadwinning: understanding men's housework in the cultural context of paid work. *Gender & Society*, 24(3): 330–54.

Thompson, L. and Walker, A.J. (1989) Gender in families: women and men in marriage, work, and parenthood. *Journal of Marriage and the Family*, 51: 845–71.

Tichenor, V.J. (2005) *Earning more and getting less: Why successful wives can't buy equality*. New Brunswick, NJ: Rutgers University Press.

Treas, J. and Drobnič, S. (2010) *Dividing the domestic: Women, men and household work in cross-national perspective*. Stanford, CA: Stanford University Press.

Twiggs, J.E., McQuillan, J., and Ferree, M.M. (1999) Meaning and measurement: reconceptualizing measures of the division of household labor. *Journal of Marriage and the Family*, 61(3): 712–24.

Umberson, D., Thomeer, M.B., and Lodge, A.C. (2015) Intimacy and emotion work in lesbian, gay, and heterosexual relationships. *Journal of Marriage and Family*, 77(2): 542–56.

Usdansky, M.L. and Parker, W.M. (2011) How money matters: college, motherhood, earnings, and wives' housework. *Journal of Family Issues*, 32(11): 1449–73.

Vespa, J., Armstrong, D.M., and Medina, L. (2018) *Demographic turning points for the United States: Population projections for 2020 to 2060*. Current Population Reports, P25-1144. Washington, DC: U.S. Census Bureau.

West, C. and Zimmerman, D.H. (1987) Doing gender. *Gender and Society*, 1: 125–51.

West, C. and Zimmerman, D.H. (2009) Accounting for doing gender. *Gender & Society*, 23: 112–22.

Wilcox, W.B. and Nock, S.L. (2006) What's love got to do with it? Equality, equity, commitment and women's marital quality. *Social Forces*, 84(3): 1321–45.

Zipp, J.F., Prohaska, A., and Bemiller, M. (2004) Wives, husbands, and hidden power in marriage. *Journal of Family Issues*, 25(7): 933–58.

# Index

www.ingramcontent.com/pod-product-compliance
Lightning Source LLC
Chambersburg PA
CBHW070931030426
42336CB00014BA/2632